A
NAZI
LEGACY

A
NAZI
LEGACY _____

Right-Wing Extremism in Postwar Germany

RAND C. LEWIS

 PRAEGER

New York
Westport, Connecticut
London

Library of Congress Cataloging-in-Publication Data

Lewis, Rand C.
    A Nazi legacy : right-wing extremism in postwar Germany /
Rand C. Lewis.
        p.   cm.
    Includes bibliographical references and index.
    ISBN 0–275–93853–0 (alk. paper)
    1. Fascism—Germany (West) 2. Germany (West)—Politics
and government—1982–   I. Title.
DD262.L48   1991
943.087—dc20   90–24277

British Library Cataloguing in Publication Data is available.

Library of Congress Catalog Card Number: 90–24277
ISBN: 0–275–93853–0

First published in 1991

Praeger Publishers, One Madison Avenue, New York, NY 10010
An imprint of Greenwood Publishing Group, Inc.

Printed in the United States of America

∞™

The paper used in this book complies with the
Permanent Paper Standard issued by the National
Information Standards Organization (Z39.48–1984).

10 9 8 7 6 5 4 3 2 1

Dedicated to
Dr. Glenn C. Lewis,
Professor Emeritus,
My father and my inspiration

Contents

Tables

Introduction

Right-wing extremism became an important domestic issue in West Germany during the 1980s. Militant rightists, associated with the extremist neo-Nazi movement, used terrorism during the first year of the decade in an attempt to emphasize the weakness of the government and to strike out against foreign influences. The West German government recognized that these neo-Nazi groups existed throughout much of the Federal Republic. However, the neo-Nazis were considered a minority faction that presented little danger to the populace, or to the political structure of the country.

The West German police quickly cracked down on those involved in the 1980 terrorist activities perpetrated by neo-Nazi associated groups or individuals. In addition, the primary neo-Nazi organizations appeared to reassess the benefits derived from the use of terrorism. As a by-product of the neo-Nazi move into the realm of terrorism, the government reevaluated the threat posed by the extreme right wing and began to place more emphasis on the tracking of separate organizations. This was especially true of those identified as neo-Nazis, who were considered to be the most susceptible to the use of terrorism as a means of attracting attention.

Neo-Nazism is not a new phenomenon in Germany. Since the end of World War II there have been numerous examples of continued pro-Nazi influences. War veterans of the Waffen

SS traditionally met for years, although these meetings were held quietly in beerhalls, with camaraderie being the primary reason given for these gatherings. Youth organizations have remained active for the past 45 years. Many of these groups were, and still are, directly related to political parties, or interests, throughout Germany. Right-wing political structures have existed in the Federal Republic of Germany since the emergence of a West German government.

The East German and West German wall was torn down in 1989 heralding major changes throughout Central Europe. Unification of the two German nations has led to still another perspective of right-wing extremist potential, both politically and domestically. Pent-up frustrations with a Communist regime that allowed no flexibility politically has led to a situation that could easily provide a basic support group for extremist right-wing political interests and, even more frightening, a foundation for terrorism.

It is important to understand the correlation of the Nazis and the presence of a modern militarist movement within West Germany, because there are so many similarities. Neo-Nazism is against the law in the Federal Republic of Germany, and yet much of the ideology associated with the Nazis and the symbols that were so effective in Hitler's rise to power were used to regenerate a nationalist fervor among a minority within Germany. Hitler himself used the crises of a broken economy, a defamed Germany—through the loss of land and power due to the Versailles Treaty—and a weak government to gain popular support for his Nazi programs. After World War II, many of those who were past members of the Nazi Party and its support organizations, such as the SS, Hitler Youth, and portions of the military, maintained an ideological attachment to the ideas of the original National Socialist German Workers Party (NSDAP). Many of these same people continued to carry elements of Nazism, such as nationalism and anti-Semitism, into their latter years. This historical precedence played a role in the development of active neo-Nazi organizations that continued to evolve over the postwar decades.

Informational material for this study came from a number of sources. The most recent and in-depth material was provided by the German Ministry of the Interior. This Ministry is responsible for the maintenance of information about organizations that may be dangerous to the political stability of the Federal Republic of Germany and insures compliance with the laws that prohibit anticonstitutional actions. These laws were invoked following World War II to provide a system of inhibiting the re-creation of organizations such as the NSDAP that would attempt to overthrow the West German government. They were designed specifically to provide a method of dealing with efforts to disrupt the constitutional rights of the citizens and to protect the people from another Nazi era. Both branches of the Interior Ministry, one located in Bonn and the other in Cologne, provided information about organizations that are on the fringe of these laws. This allowed them to track the radical groups' growth and influence. The government report, *Verfassungsschutzbericht*, was prepared annually since the early 1970s. This report initially covered terrorist actions on the left, but since the early 1980s included those actions on the right that appeared to endanger the stability of West German society. This source provided excellent statistical data that showed the trends in radical militarism.

A special study was conducted for the West German government in 1979 and the early 1980s. This study was completed by a number of academics in Germany and was designed to provide information to help counter the terrorist threat that had been prevalent since the 1960s. Divided into five volumes, the study analyzed the ideologies and strategies of the different radical groups, the types of people active in terrorism, and developed a statistical analysis of the psychological aspects of the terrorists.[1] Although these sources tend to emphasize the left-wing threat of terrorism, a fair amount of recent information was gathered about the right wing.

Militant excesses by right-wing extremists were reported extensively in newspapers. Numerous incidents of harassment, theft, murder, and neo-Nazi rallies have surfaced since early 1980. Cases of neo-Nazis painting graffiti on the homes of foreigners, bombing facilities that house foreigners, and instances of organized neo-Nazi gatherings were reported in a number of the local papers. Many of these occurrences were covered by both German news sources and international network agencies. These news sources provided fairly reliable descriptions of those events that the government often attributed to the right-wing radicals, normally classified as neo-Nazi elements. These news stories identified those individuals, or groups, who participated in the illegal acts, thereby providing a method of tracking activities in which right-wing extremists were involved.

Historians and political scientists from both Germany and the United States included some data on the German right-wing extremists in many of their writings. Those who write about terrorism showed a greater interest in the subject over the past ten years, commensurate with the increase in right-wing extremist activity. Kurt Tauber, a German historian, developed a fairly extensive search of post-World War II right-wing organizations that were active from 1946 to 1965. Tauber wrote a two-volume book for researchers, which included a large bibliography and a fairly in-depth discussion of the different nationalist organizations that were formed during the 20 years following the war. Although these volumes cover all of the groups that developed on the right during this period, they offer excellent examples of the vast number of organizations, both political and youth, that continued the tradition of nationalism. Most of these groups stayed within the limits of the law. Many, however, remained close to the edge of the law and tended to lean heavily toward the old Nazi ideologies of the prewar period. Groups such as the Socialist Reich Party (SRP), that drifted too far to the right, became casualties of the anti-Nazi laws of both the Allied occupation authorities and the emerging West German government. As these right-wing groups drifted beyond the limits of the law and the constitution, they were deemed illegal and a danger to the new German system. What became of the members of these outlawed organizations? They often joined other rightist groups or instituted a new political party that maintained similar ideologies, but was accepted by the government. Not until the late 1970s did the rise of the rightist extremists cause the government to consider the effects of these groups working outside of the laws.

Gordon Craig, in his social history of Germany, *The Germans*, provided additional insight into the growing problem of right-wing radicalism. He suggested that although the extremists only make up a minor part of the population, their "shouting of old slogans tend to be disheartening to the majority of the West German population."[2] In addition, Craig supports the thesis that since 1978 the West German government deemed it necessary to follow more closely the activities of the professed neo-Nazi groups.

There were a number of studies about terrorism completed over the past 15 years, which included some references to right-wing militancy. Such authors as Walter Laqueur, Paul Wilkinson, and Jonah Alexander, all known for their work in studies of terrorism, provided some insight into the rising neo-Nazi phenomenon. Since most of the activity involving terrorism in Europe has been associated with the left wing, the right wing remained fairly innocuous until events in 1980. This led many experts, prior to 1980, to conclude that the militant right wing was not a valid threat. Only after the bombings in 1980, and the beginnings of overt activity by neo-Nazi groups in Europe and the United States, was there any consideration that a threat may exist. Even these events were most often portrayed as isolated actions that were of little importance.

Although some references to right-wing extremism were included in a number of writings, actual studies that specifically address the rise of right-wing militancy in Europe, particularly in Germany, were, and still are, severely limited. Other than data collection, group identification, and a general knowledge that these groups existed, or still exist, little was written expressly about this subject. In general, during the first 30 years following World War II academic interest in right-wing extremist activities was limited. Only during the past ten years was more information about the extent of the activities and membership of these groups made available. This increased information made the subject a more viable area of study. The reasons for this increase in information was twofold. First, the numbers of extremists that were apprehended by the police for increasingly more severe crimes provided the government agencies with a valuable source of information. Second, the apparent disregard for the anti-Nazi laws that were promulgated by West Germany following the war, led to an open flaunting of the old Nazi slogans and methods, which graphically reminded the Europeans that Nazism had not disappeared.

NOTES

1. These studies are generically placed under the title, *Analysen zum Terrorismus*, Hrsg. v. Bundesministerium des Innern. The following three volumes are excellent sources that include right-wing data: I. Fetscher and G. Rohrmoser, *Ideologien und Strategien* (Opladen: Westdeutscher Verlag GmbH, 1981); H. Jäger, G. Schmidtchen, and L. Süllwold, *Lebenslaufanalysen* (Opladen: Westdeutscher Verlag GmbH, 1981); W. Baeyer-Katte et al., *Gruppenprozesse* (Opladen: Westdeutscher Verlag GmbH, 1982). Commissioned by the West German government, these studies used government documentation to provide an in-depth look at terrorism and those that participated in acts of terrorism in Germany.

2. Gordon A. Craig, *The Germans* (New York: G. P. Putnam's Sons, 1982), 80.

1   The Past Revisited

We don't want higher bread prices!
We don't want lower bread prices!
We want National Socialist bread prices!

George L. Mosse, *Masses and Man*, 164.

Hitler's suicide in the Berlin bunker on April 30, 1945, signaled the end to World War II and an apparent finale to the Nazi Party. The National Socialist German Workers Party (NSDAP), commonly known as the Nazi Party, ruled Germany for over twelve years. Hitler's dream of German domination in Europe and *lebensraum* in the East for the German population, coupled with his insistence on German racial purity, provided the basis for the Nazi program. However, the strong German nationalism that permeated a segment of the population was not eliminated by Hitler's suicide, nor by the Allied occupation of war-torn Germany following the defeat of the Third Reich.

Many of the right-wing extremists, often with Nazi backgrounds, carried some of the most potent Nazi ideologies forward over the four decades following the war. These ideologies became the mainstays of the neo-Nazi groups of the 1980s. The neo-Nazi movements reinstituted such concepts as racial purity, German nationalism and dominance, responses to wartime losses, and identification of a common enemy, which Germans could blame for their economic woes.

Racial purity was an important element of Hitler's plan for a "great" Germany. This was shown repeatedly in his speeches and was included in his book, *Mein Kampf.* Of course, the Nazis emphasized the need to eliminate the Jews and the "*Untermenschen*," which were identified as the peoples of the Eastern European and Russian regions.

The emphases of present-day neo-Nazis are on the Turkish immigrants, along with some anti-Semitic activities, such as defacing Jewish buildings and monuments. What is important about this desire to isolate and persecute foreigners and Jews is that both the Nazis and the neo-Nazis used minorities to justify acts of terrorism. The Jews and Turks, targeted during different periods in history, were blamed for problems that existed in Germany. For example, the Nazis charged the Jews with being the instigators of the financial debacle during the 1920s and early 1930s. In addition, Hitler argued that many of the political and domestic problems that existed during the Weimar period were attributed directly to Jewish influences. During the 1980s, the economic woes and unemployment experienced by the "blue collar" portion of the West German population provided the impetus for the neo-Nazis and right-wing radical political parties, Republikaner (REP) and Nationaldemokratische Partei Deutschland (NPD), to once again blame minorities within Germany. The Turks, who moved into West Germany to find jobs, most of which were menial, became targets of right-wing propaganda. Many of the right-wing extremists, including the neo-Nazis, claimed that the Turks directly contributed to the high rate of unemployment, which ran about 8 percent during 1988 and early 1989.

During both the Nazi period and the more recent neo-Nazi period, attempts to blame others for the systemic problems within Germany brought about an opportunity to gain popular support politically. This was initially shown in the election results of 1932, when the Nazi Party garnered over 33 percent (37.3 percent in early 1932 and 33.1 percent in later 1932) of the popular vote. The modern right-wing extremists, strongly supported by the neo-Nazis, used the arguments against foreigners in the 1989 state elections in West Berlin and Hesse, where right-wing candidates obtained eleven and three seats respectfully in local parliaments. This is not to say that the NSDAP in the 1930s was able to obtain such popular support purely by blaming a minority, but the rhetoric they used hammered on the unfairness of the Versailles Treaty, the failure of the Weimar government, and the need to reestablish Germany's borders. Inherent in these arguments was the underlying position that the Jews were responsible for many of Germany's ills.

Although the right-wing extremists, including the neo-Nazis, were able to obtain a following in the recent 1989 elections, a strong anti-Nazi feeling permeated the German political structure throughout the postwar period. West German reactions following the elections showed that a major portion of the present West German population, and their political representatives, still carried anti-Nazi feelings.

This was evidenced by the controversy resulting from a speech given in a special memorial session of the West German Parliament in 1988 commemorating the Jews that had suffered on *Kristallnacht*.[1] Philipp Jenninger, a member of the Christian Democratic Party (CDU), the moderate conservative right party that represents a major portion of the fairly conservative German population, delivered the speech on November 10, 1988. Jenninger attempted to show that most Germans let themselves be "blinded and seduced" by the Nazis in the 1930s.[2] His speech emphasized the German responsibility for the Jewish pogrom, but then Jenninger provided an analysis of the mood of many of the Germans in the 1930s. He quoted a hypothetical man-in-the-street asking himself whether "the Jews not perhaps deserved to be put in their place?"[3] This analogy was poorly accepted by many members of the parliament, particularly those members of the rival Socialist Democratic Party of Germany (SPD), which represents the leftist and liberal electorate within West Germany. The initial reaction from the media was speculation over whether these were true feelings of the speaker or was he only using an example. Although the final verdict was one of exoneration, it did not help Jenninger who was forced to resign. The outcry from both liberals and conservatives showed that any semblance of support of the Nazi regime, or attempts at justifying the purposes of the Nazi era, were still inappropriate. The furor raised over the Jenninger speech indicated that there was still a sensitivity in dealing with the Nazi past.[4]

In other developments within West Germany, government officials claimed in late 1988 that neo-Nazi computer buffs were spreading militant propaganda through rewritten computer game software.[5] These methods of spreading Nazi propaganda to the youth of West Germany are difficult to control and therefore provided a new source of neo-Nazi information. The West German government's concerns were heightened by this fearsome new avenue of disseminating neo-Nazi propaganda.[6]

The responses to Nazi references provide an insight into the sensitivity and apparent hostility on the part of the West Germans concerning neo-Nazism. The German Parliament representatives' negative responses, and the public outcry against Jenninger's speech, were indicative of the growing concerns within West Germany over extremists, particularly those supporting neo-Nazi interests that exist on the fringes of West German politics and society.[7]

Interest in the evolution of right-wing militancy in both the United States and Europe has been fairly limited over the past two decades in comparison to that of the left-wing. The reasons for this are difficult to ascertain. However, there are indications that the right wing, particularly in West Germany, has retained such a low profile over the years that the more militant elements have not been deemed important enough to cause fears of returned Nazism. An often quoted Hughes Mearns poem, "The Psychoed," can be used to portray the frustrations involved in following the growing international neo-Nazi movement. The poem symbolizes the relationship of human reaction to perception. In the first stanza, Mearns suggests that reactions are often an attempt to deny the existence of a situation, although it is perceived to exist, or, in fact, does exist.

Many people are aware of the fringe extremists that have become known in many parts of the world as neo-Nazis. The crushing of Hitler's Third Reich in the mid-1940s was considered by many to have been the death knoll for viable fascism. Today's neo-Nazi is often presumed to be an extremist ultra-conservative, who uses historical symbolism of the German Third Reich and devout nationalism to lend an air of authority to modern extremist interests. Their numbers, although minute, still provide a sense of fear among those who remember the rise of Nazism in the 1920s and 1930s. Officially, neo-Nazism is a minor irritant that brings back memories of world war and death, and is specifically outlawed by the German constitution. Unofficially, the revival of Nazi sloganism and xenophobia among a minority within the national populations of Europe have caused a great amount of consternation among governments and peoples that still carry vivid memories of Hitler's era. Although the "man on the stair" may not be considered an immediate danger, the haunting realization that he exists strikes a certain amount of fear into those who have heard similar rhetoric before.

Modern German right-wing militants evolved from the threads of nationalism, protectionism, and fascism that dominated Italy and Germany from the 1920s until the mid-1940s, and permeated European countries occupied by Hitler's and Mussolini's forces during the war. The defeat of Hitler's Third Reich in 1945 presumably resulted in the disintegration of the Nazi ideology. However, where did the neo-Nazis of the 1970s and 1980s come from? Was this a reemergence of the Nazi ideology that was carried forward by previous participants in Hitler's organizations? Or was this a new style of nationalism that developed in response to the changes in Germany brought on by the events of the 1960s and 1970s? In an attempt to answer these basic questions, the right wing in Germany since 1945 must be considered and evaluated for the common threads that tie the militants of the Right together. The right wing encompasses a large number of groups within West Germany, numbering in excess of 400. Therefore, it is necessary to focus on the extremist groups that are most closely associated with the ideological interests of the Nazi Party of pre-1945. This, of course, is best represented by the modern neo-Nazi movements that became far more visible during the early 1980s. By definition, right-wing extremism refers to those individuals within Germany—both West and East—who are the most radical of the ultra-conservative nationalists. These people often associate with the more moderate right-wing supporters through the conservative parties, such as the Christian Democratic Union (CDU) and Christian Socialist Union (CSU), but do not hesitate to support far more radical methods, such as force, to obtain power or guide Germany's future.

What constitutes right-wing extremism in Germany and what are the susceptibilities for using terrorism? Table 1.1 provides an analysis of the best known right-wing organizations that exist in West Germany, which includes political parties and radical militant organizations. The German right-wing traditionally attracted conservatives, whether they were monarchists, nationalists, or supporters of movements or ideals that espoused traditional German (*Völkisch*) values. A good number of the postwar population moved toward moderate conservatism due to the fear of socialism and liberalization of traditional values.

The Christian Democratic Union (CDU), along with its Bavarian counterpart, the Christian Socialist Union (CSU), provided the moderate conservative political parties that were most acceptable for the conservative elements in West Germany following the war. Other right-wing organizations extended to the right of the CDU/CSU, in varying degrees of extremism and radicalism. The neo-Nazis are considered the most extreme. These groups were known to have used physical violence, harassment, and illegal use of Nazi symbolism to further their ideological goals. Inherent in a definition of German right-wing extremism is the inclusion of those individuals who used illegal means of activity, such as criminal actions, and espoused the strong right-wing nationalist ideology. The West German government used the appellation "neo-Nazi" because many of these organizations assumed historical Nazi symbols, ideologies, and militarism. These included the use of outlawed Nazi symbols (i.e., the swastika), the belief in racism (in some cases anti-Semitism), the pursuit of military training, and pan-Germanism. Therefore, when identifying right-wing extremism in West Germany, the entire spectrum of right wing that exists beyond the legally acceptable conservative political order is included. The extent of illegality, or fanaticism, varies with each group. Some remained on the very edge of West

Table 1.1
Right-Wing Extremism Versus Terrorism

Least Extreme	-Christian Social Union (CDU/CSU)	Conservative Political Parties
	-National Democratic Party (NPD)	Extreme RW Political Party
Moderate	-Democratic Reich Party (DRP)	Ultra-Conservative Party in Lower Saxony (merged w/NPD in 1964)
	-Socialist Reich Party (SRP)	RW Extremist Party (banned in 1952)
	-Freiheitliche Deutsche Arbeiterpartei (FAP)	Neo-Nazi group which boasted largest membership in 1988. (uses political system)
Militant	-Frei Arbeiter Partei	Spinoff from militant ANS-NA. (supports political methods)
	-Deutsche Aktionsgruppe (DA)	Neo-Nazi group organized by Manfred Roeder
Most Militant	-Wehrsportgruppen Hoffman	Neo-Nazi group organized by Karl Heinz Hoffman (defunct-1988)
	-Aktionsgemeinschaft Nationaler Sozialisten-Nationale Aktivisten (ANS-NA)	Extremely militant neo-Nazi group under the leadership of Michael Kühnen
	-Hilfsorganization für Nationale Politische Gefangene und deren Angehörige e.V. (HNG)	Small neo-Nazi group with a reputation for extreme militancy
	-Arbeitsgemeinschaft Nationaler -Verbände/Völkischer Bund (ANV/VB)	Virulent neo-Nazi group which targets U.S. and NATO Forces

German law, retaining a facade of legality, such as the National Democratic Party of Germany (NPD), and yet consistently supported the more militant elements that existed on their fringes. Others, such as the Wehrsportgruppen Hoffman and the groups that were organized by Michael Kühnen and Manfred Roeder, went beyond the edge of legality and developed the most ardent right-wing militant groups that were not afraid to use terrorism to obtain their goals.

The numbers of right-wing extremists are minimal in comparison to the overall population of West Germany. The government estimated a total number of identified right-wing extremists at around 25,000 in 1988.[8] Of this number, less than 10 percent were identified as neo-Nazis.[9] These numbers appear to diminish the importance of the right-wing extremists. The visibility of these neo-Nazi groups becomes more evident to the Germans, however, when their actions are highlighted by the news media.

West German officials recognized the potentially dangerous trend of right-wing extremism during the late 1970s. The neo-Nazi groups showed more aggressive activity and provided a more susceptible political climate for the extremist right-wing political parties, such as the Republikaner and the NPD, to expand their power base. The government was forced to re-evaluate right-wing influence on the West Germans because of the more strident and openly aggressive extremist activities, such as the terrorist acts of the 1980s, the international neo-Nazi connections, and the development of a more viable political arm. Through the use of commissioned studies, the Ministry of the Interior began to piece together the history and backgrounds of the neo-Nazi organizations. A group of radicals that, until the late 1970s, were considered to be a minor nuisance became a viable problem for German society. This led the government to pursue a new approach in dealing with the growing, albeit small, militant neo-Nazi movement.

Both the moderate left and right were afforded the opportunity to develop politically in the Federal Republic of Germany after 1946. Democratic government also provided opportunities for radical development, which was evidenced by the growth of militant groups such as the left-wing Red Army

Faction (RAF) and the right-wing neo-Nazis. A number of political parties organized over the 40 years following the political autonomy granted by the Allies. Many of the early parties were unable to attract support and therefore were short-lived. Others adjusted to the changing times and were able to retain different levels of support over the four decades. In the case of two parties, the Socialist Reich Party (SRP) and the Communist Party (KPD), the West German government deemed them to be outside the laws of the new Republic, and therefore banned them. All of these political entities, whether they met the minimum requirement of 5 percent of the popular vote or not, maintained a semblance of a following from either the right, left, or center. The majority of the postwar West German population traditionally supported the moderate liberalism of the Social Democratic Party (SPD) or the moderate conservatism of the Christian Democratic Party (CDU). As is the case in many Western democracies, there were those who also supported more extreme socialist, or communist, ideologies. On the other hand, there were those who supported the more conservative, or nationalist ideas, as well.

Within the major political parties of the SPD and CDU/CSU there are different political views. Members of these parties share a common political goal for their party platform, but many support their own specific interests, which are subordinated to the general good of the party. The smaller political entities, such as the Free Democratic Party (FDP), which became more of a centrist party in the 1970s, the National Democratic Party of Germany (NPD), often referred to by opponents as the neo-Nazi Party, the Communist Party (DKP), and the Green Party, provide alternatives to the West German voters. Although these smaller parties do not carry the prestige, nor power, of the two large moderate parties, their influence is still felt in German politics. Often, a coalition between the major party and one, or more, of the minor parties is needed in order for one party to gain control of the government. This arrangement lends to the legitimizing of the smaller parties.

The traditional linkage of the CDU and the Bavarian conservative party, Christian Socialist Union (CSU), is the coalition of importance to the right wing. For many years, the

CSU, under the leadership of Franz Josef Strauss,[10] provided a strong conservative support base for the rest of the moderate conservatives who supported the CDU throughout West Germany.

If one was looking at the right wing graphically, it would be best to consider the CDU/CSU as the moderate point at the left side of a right-wing scale. Right-wing extremism begins on the right-hand fringe of the CDU/CSU and proceeds to the right until reaching the most militant and extreme right-wingers, the neo-Nazis. Right-wing extremist sympathizers often hover around the fringe of these moderate conservative, or nationalist parties. These radical rightists tend to differ with the majority of the party membership when dealing with national interests and Germanism. Many of these people support a more aggressive policy for elimination of occupying forces and the reunification of Germany. The more militant the organizations, the more aggressive are the actions against those who disagree with the extremist's positions.

It is important to point out that, although a small portion of the German population today has sympathies with many of the right-wing extremist's views, particularly dealing with foreign workers, the support for the neo-Nazis remains extremely limited. The neo-Nazis, on the other hand, used the commonalities of interests between themselves and the less militant extremists to obtain support and new members from other right-wing groups. The best example of this was the support received in the 1989 Hessian state elections, where the Turkish immigrants became a major issue for right-wing adherents throughout Germany. In this case, the neo-Nazis actively campaigned for the NPD candidates, many of whom won seats in this state parliament election.

The increase in right-wing political power, which galvanized the most radical elements of the right wing, portends to open a new chapter in German political history. Although this increase in political power was predicated on a popular fear of the foreign influences, the extremist right remains a small minority within West Germany. The key question revolves around the extent to which the extremists are willing to go in order to further their ideological goals. It is therefore important that the continuation of Nazi ideology, as used by the neo-

Nazis, be more succinctly understood and that the potential threat be considered with more circumspection. Since the early 1980s, the militancy of the neo-Nazis, particularly in West Germany and the United States, shifted from harassment and threats to more aggressive actions that included robbery, physical attacks, and murder.

In order to understand the continuation of the Nazi legacy through the evolution of neo-Nazi groups, it is important to deal with the questions of whether these neo-Nazi groups pose a threat and why they continue to emerge. There appear to be substantial personal connections between generations of right-wing nationalists and ex-Nazis, but the ramifications and extent of these connections are difficult to ascertain. In addition, cooperation with international neo-Nazi groups and terrorist supporting organizations, such as the Palestinian Liberation Organization (PLO), provided support in training, material, and morale, which allowed the radicals to develop into terrorist threats.

Within the United States, a belief that Nazism was crushed at the end of World War II provided the basis for deemphasizing the potential of modern neo-Nazism. This did not suggest that the United States was totally unaware of right-wing extremism in West Germany. From 1945 to the late 1970s, the extremists were able to evolve quietly, often without undue pressure from the governments. Many officials within the U.S. government felt that the chances of right-wing extremism blossoming into more than a minor underground were extremely limited. The death of Hitler, the denazification program—an effort on the part of the United States to eliminate Nazism throughout the Allied zone of occupation in Germany—and the development of a democratic political system in Germany provided the foundation for this attitude. In addition, the obvious threat posed by the left-wing activists in Europe, particularly during the 1970s, took precedence over the right-wing extremists, who appeared impotent.

NEO-NAZI ROOTS

The roots of right-wing extremism in postwar Germany began with the Nazi Party of the 1920s. Nazism provided a basic militaristic political ideology, some of which became identified with the right-wing extremists during the four decades following the World War II. The continuation of militarism, pan-Germanism, racial purity, and the use of propaganda combined with symbolism, were important elements associated with the prewar Nazis and postwar rightist militant movements.

The Neo-Nazis, during the late 1970s and early 1980s, epitomized the return of the right-wing extremists to the prewar Nazi ideology and methods. As was the case with the failure of the National Socialist Party to force change by violent rebellion in 1923, the neo-Nazis found that violence was not the most desirable method of achieving political change in the early 1980s. The use of violence, or terrorism, was found to be counterproductive in both cases, leading both groups to reevaluate their methods for obtaining their goals. Upon reconsideration, each found that the most viable procedure was to use the existing political system. However, each retained their capability for armed aggression. This was best shown by the stockpiling of arms and munitions by the Nazi SA organizations during the 1920s and the neo-Nazis of the 1980s.

Similarities between the Nazi Party and the present-day neo-Nazis are hauntingly familiar. Right-wing extremists of the postwar period carried the label of Nazis, but the neo-Nazis were the epitome of this identity. Extremists were considered to have Nazi leanings due to the fact that many of the leaders had backgrounds associated with Nazi organizations, such as the party political arm, paramilitary force, youth groups, or military. Many of these extremists, although often tempering their pro-Nazi interests and activities, remained on the far right of West German politics. A small number of these men moved into the militant organizations that became known as the neo-Nazis. These ex-Nazis provided support and, in some cases, leadership to the neo-Nazi movement, which flaunted the traditions of such Nazi organizations as the SA and SS. This continuation of Nazi ideology is the embodiment of the relationship between modern Germany and its turbulent past.

The basic foundation for postwar neo-Nazi support was laid by the NSDAP under the tutelage of Hitler. Historically, the rise to power of the Nazi Party was predicated upon a series of unique events that afforded the opportunity for a support base. Postwar trauma, economic collapse, high unemployment, and a need to search for German identity were ingredients for a radical change. Using methods combining rhetoric and violence, the NSDAP gained a foothold in the political structure of Germany.

Needless to say, the Germany of the 1990s does not compare to Germany of the 1920s. However, many of the same tactics that Hitler's party and the modern right-wing militants used are strikingly similar. The arguments for nationalism, German purity, and German unity remain the same. Historically, the roots of modern neo-Nazism appear to be closely associated with those of the 1920s and 1930s.

The National Socialist German Workers Party (NSDAP) evolved during a period of intense instability in Germany in the early 1920s. The party was organized in Munich and was one of a number of right-wing groups that had been organized throughout Germany in response to difficult economic times and defeat in World War I. The NSDAP was originally called the German Workers Party and began with a total active membership of seven. Hitler's assumption of power in the party was based on his personal qualities. His unique speaking abilities and his capability to organize and provide effective propaganda methods made him indispensable to the party.[11] By April 1, 1920, the German Worker's Party was renamed the National Socialist German Worker's Party. This renaming was in conjunction with the acceptance of a 25-point program that Hitler and one of the original organizers of the German Worker's Party, Anton Drexler, wrote during the early organizational period of the party. These articles set down the basic positions for the continuation and growth of the party.

The 25 points demanded the union of all Germans in Greater Germany, provided an appeal for support from the lower classes, called for the abrogation of the Treaties of Versailles and St. Germain, and the creation of a strong central power of the state.[12] In addition, the document required that unearned income be abolished, large industries nationalized, and that there be land reform.[13] There were eight provisions dealing with anti-Semitism. The drafters of the document insured that

Jews could not be citizens, nor even live in Germany except as guests who came under alien laws. Therefore, Jewish ownership was severely limited, offices were prohibited, and in the event of food shortages, the Jews were to be expelled. During the early years of the party, Hitler believed that a strong nationalist Germany, predicated on a party based on the working classes, was essential in overcoming the weak democratic Republic that the right-wing perceived was leading Germany to disaster. Therefore, membership efforts were initially designed to obtain the support of the lower classes.

Through Hitler's efforts, the party membership grew. Monies flowed into the party coffers as paid attendance at the NSDAP meetings increased. Hitler's speeches drew increasingly larger crowds, as he used his natural speaking abilities to attract interest. His importance to the organization became paramount to the survival of the fledgling party. An early attempt to eliminate Hitler as a potential usurper of the party leadership was thwarted when Hitler offered to resign. The resignation would have fractured the newly developing party.[14] In essence, this attempt gave Hitler the opportunity to solidify his position and to provide him with dictatorial powers within the party.

Initially, the right-wing parties throughout Germany provided an outlook for those who felt that the German soldier had been "stabbed in the back" by government officials at the end of World War I. This feeling that the Treaty of Versailles was an affront to the fighting men was promulgated by Hitler and the NSDAP. The outcome of this program of propaganda was the increase in support from veterans, many of whom were displaced and unable to adjust to a new Germany at peace. These men often joined military groups called *Freikorps* (Free Corps), which became important assets to the right-wing revolutionists. Members of the Free Corps, along with a growing membership in paramilitary leagues of unemployed youth, waged a civil war against those who were perceived to have failed Germany in the war. German National Socialism provided a basic ideology and the support that appealed to many of these disenchanted men.

In the summer of 1920, Hitler organized the *Ordnertruppe*, which were basically strong-arm squads made up of war veterans. This first "protection" organization was placed under the leadership of Emil Maurice, an ex-convict.[15] These ex-servicemen were initially used to silence hecklers and, if necessary, toss the troublemakers out of party meetings. The government realized the potency of these organizations but were initially afraid to ban such militant groups. The reasons for this apparent oversight were twofold. The Reich government feared the loss of votes in Bavaria and therefore a weakening of the already shaky Republican coalition. In addition, the instability of the government forced the politicians to show good will to the Bavarians in order to quell separatist tendencies. Prussia, on the other hand, showed little interest in Hitler's growing popularity in Bavaria. Hitler was forbidden to speak in Prussia for years, therefore, the Nazi formations were ineffective in the Prussian state until after 1930.

The NSDAP camouflaged their squads as the "Gymnastic and Sports Division."[16] By October 1921, this NSDAP protection group was renamed the *Sturmsabteilung*, more commonly known as the SA. Free Corps members were actively recruited and used to break up opposition group meetings. This use of paramilitary force was employed to exploit the weaknesses of the Weimar republic government.[17] Hitler was explicit in stating that these SA forces were not allowed to have any affiliation with the then popular military organizations called "defense leagues."[18] He also argued that the SA was not to be a secret organization, and that the Party "must drive home to the Marxist that the future master of the streets will be National Socialism, exactly as some day it will be the master of the State."[19]

The development of the militant side of the right wing within the NSDAP tended to give the party a radical flare. This militancy became most evident in the attempted "Beer Hall *Putsch*" of 1923. This was Hitler's attempt at obtaining power through the use of force, which resulted in failure. This premature use of force set the precedent for the methods that Hitler followed from 1923 until obtaining power in 1933. No longer was the key to gaining power predicated on military revolution but on political maneuvering. He used a mixture of intense slogans and nationalist mythology, similar to Mussolini's methods, to woo the support of the German masses.

The NSDAP used the ten years following the failed *Putsch* for revitalization and growth. A number of historians over the past 40 years have pondered the question of how the NSDAP rose above the other right-wing parties and survived to become the dominant party in Germany. Some writers, such as William Shirer, argued that Nazism was the logical continuation of German history. James D. Forman, in his book *Nazism*, suggested that Hitler "was the extreme expression of generations of German thinking and feeling."[20]

Other historians, such as Maurice Baumont, argued that Nazism evolved from events that followed World War I.[21] The basic premise for this popular interpretation of events is that Hitler used a cry for nationalism to overcome the shame of the Treaty of Versailles. Once the NSDAP developed a substantial power base, the weakened Weimar government was prey to the Nazi propaganda machine. Worsening economic conditions strengthened the Nazi Party's position among the population. The NSDAP offered a program that would presumably return Germany to a viable European power and reestablish employment opportunities and self-esteem within Germany. Hitler's use of modern means of communications was an important method of reaching the majority. Albert Speer, one of Hitler's trusted lieutenants, said that Hitler "controlled the German population through modern technological means, such as radio and films."[22]

The question of whether or not the Nazi legacy was hidden within German history has been hotly debated for over 40 years. What is clear is that the inter-war years from 1918 to 1939 were extremely difficult for Germany. Nationalism was not new to Europe in the early 1900s. Fascism was identified as an alternative to the old monarchies, socialism, and the new liberal democracies. Within German society were the rising fears of the old "elite," who foresaw the potential decline of their power and prestige as democracy supplanted the monarchies. Worldwide depression forced thousands into abject poverty and hopelessness. The physical damage throughout Germany that was caused by war, as well as the damage to the population's psyche, tended to erode self-confidence. All of these factors provided an opportunity for radicalism to develop and grow. This radicalism, as implemented by the National Socialists, portrayed itself as the answer to the problems and having the ability to bring stability.

As the Nazis attempted to develop their power base, Hitler began to realize that the lower working class was not a viable group for right-wing sympathies. The reason for not readily obtaining the lower class support was related to the inability of the Nazis to meet the needs of the "blue-collar" worker. The SPD and Communist parties were far more acceptable to this group of people. These two parties based their entire program on the needs of the working class, thereby best representing this class of German society. Hitler's organization employed concepts such as racial elitism, anti-Semitism, land reform, and nationalism that were not as appealing to the lower classes, who were attempting to survive in economic collapse. The middle class, which included the small businessmen, farmers, and local "white-collar" workers, became the focal point for Nazi propaganda. In general, the German middle class was not as overtly affected by the economic failures and unemployment as the lower classes.[23] What prompted a reconsideration of political interests within the middle class were principally perceptions. Members of this class were affected by the spiraling inflation, as savings and inheritances became less valuable. But the everyday survival problems that were inherent in the blue-collar portions of German society were far less apparent in the white-collar and farm portions. The perception that they would be facing the hard times like other people in Germany caused the middle class to seek a political solution from the growing NSDAP. A growing distrust of the government among this class provided fertile ground for the Nazis to obtain membership and to draw the power from the center parties. The government fueled this distrust by increasing the effort to stem unemployment and financial ruin in industry. By instituting "welfare state" supports, such as the 48-hour week, wage controls, and workplace participation, the Weimar government was viewed by a large portion of the middle class as being too closely allied with the labor unions.[24]

Traditionally, labor was considered lower class in German society. The apparent support provided by the government was

perceived by the other classes as a threat to the traditional
social system. This led to growing support for the Nazis, who
used an extensive number of slogans and programs that harped
on the middle class fears. Workers remained largely uncom-
mitted politically during the late 1920s, whereas the middle
class became more adamant supporters of the NSDAP.[25]

Not only did the small town lower middle class become the
basic foundation for the Nazi movement, but the rural population tended to lean toward the NSDAP. The general cross-
section of National Socialist membership in 1930 indicated a
minimum of unionization.[26] These members were primarily
farm workers, railroad workers, postal and civil service employees, small to medium tradesmen, and youth. The majority
were not only middle class, but were predominantly Protestant.
In September 1930, the Nazi Party membership was composed
of approximately 26.3 percent of the working class.[27] Of the
total party membership, 24 percent were white collar, 13.2
percent were farmers, 18.9 percent were self-employed, 7.7 percent were civil service, and 9.9 percent were other.[28] Although
the total middle class was not committed to the NSDAP, a
number of the rural and small community population showed
tendencies toward supporting the nationalism and anticom-
munist ideology of Hitler and his Nazi Party.

By the time Hitler assumed power in 1933, the foundation
of the NSDAP was dominated by the middle class, and supported by an increasing number of blue-collar workers who had
found no economic respite in other organizations. The Nazis
were forced to redirect their efforts in order to obtain the support of the working class. Not until after 1930 did the working
class forsake the socialist groups and begin to join the Nazi
Party in appreciable numbers. In early 1933, over one-third of
the NSDAP membership was comprised of workers, craftsmen,
farm laborers, and civil servants.[29] On the contrary, only a
minority of the membership was made up of bureaucrats,
professional intelligentsia, and capital-possessing elements.[30]
Between 1930 and 1933, approximately 720,000 new members
joined the NSDAP.[31] Forty-three percent of this new membership was under 30 years of age and were from traditionally
liberal or conservative middle class families.[32] This was a move-

ment that attracted the younger generation, particularly as the economic situation continued to look bleaker. Unemployment increased from 1,368,000 to 3,144,000 between 1929 and 1930.[33] By 1931, this number grew to 5,668,000 and then by 1932 exceeded 6 million.[34]

The NSDAP successes during the late 1930s with the middle class hinged on the needs of that class within society. The Nazis agreed to maintain the traditional system relating to property ownership. This was key to obtaining the farmer and the urban middle class support. In addition, the NSDAP offered those of the middle class a political force that was radical enough to liquidate the existing political system that was unable to guarantee order.

Results of the *Reichstag* elections from 1920 through 1932 graphically show the rate of popular growth that the Nazi Party experienced. In May 1924, the NSDAP captured 6.5 percent of the popular vote.[35] Between the December 1924 and the 1928 elections, there was a steady decline, which was primarily due to an organizational and political disunity that plagued the party.[36] By September 1930, the Nazis began a credible resurgence polling 18.3 percent of the popular vote, up from 2.6 percent in 1928.[37] Elections in July 1932 indicated a doubling of support with a 37.3 percent of the popular vote.[38] The final elections in November 1932 showed another drop in support to 33.1 percent (Table 1.2). The rapidity of the rise in electoral support was indicative of Nazi efforts to gain a power base in the middle and working classes. Using a carrot-and-stick combination the party was able to control numerous rural and small town environments. They offered a party that had a specific goal and, therefore, could feasibly bring back a semblance of stability. On the other hand, the Nazis used strong-arm tactics to give the population a sense that the NSDAP was capable of physical, as well as, political strength.

By 1929, a number of small groups, or cells, of Nazis had emerged throughout eastern central Germany. Initially, these groups were predominantly composed of individuals who were displeased with the outcome of World War I or wanted to develop a strong patriotic solidarity that would replace the rigid, traditional class distinctions.[39] Both of these types of partici-

Table 1.2
German Election Results, 1930–1932

	Sep 1932	July 1932	Nov 1932
NSDAP	18.3%	37.8%	33.1%
Nationalists (DNVP, Landvölk, Peasant Party, Landbund)	11.5%	6.6%	9.6%
Total Right-wing	29.8%	44.4%	42.7%
SPD	24.5%	21.6%	20.0%
Communists	13.1%	14.6%	16.9%
Center Party (Catholic)-disbanded in July 1933	32.6%	19.8%	20.0%
% non-voting	18.6%	16.6%	20.1%

March 5, 1933 election-43.9% voted with the NSDAP and 7.9% voted with other Nationalist parties. The other nationalists were incorporated into the NSDAP in July, 1933.

pants tended to be middle class. Ultimately, with the inclusion of members from the rural regions and the artisan trades, the rightist organizations dominated the local social life. Many of the middle class joined the local NSDAP in the early years in order to insure social justice, or as a hedge against unemployment.

The ranks of the Ruhr NSDAP were also filled by young people, most of whom were between the ages of 23 and 33.[40] The party offered an outlet for unemployment frustrations and an opportunity to identify with a strong nationalist organization. The appeal of paramilitary slogans, uniforms, and discipline offered many the opportunity to develop a sense of control over their environment.

Johnpeter Horst Grill, in his book *The Nazi Movement in Baden, 1920–1945*, portrays the evolution of Nazi strength in an area fairly close to Munich, which was the birthplace of the NSDAP. Once again, the initial beginnings of the local party chapter were led by influence of returning veterans. These veterans became the farmers and artisans of the town of Baden. The younger men quickly became dissatisfied with the town fathers' traditional conservative methods of handling the many problems associated with the rebuilding of Germany and the local region.[41] The increase in Baden membership in the NSDAP between 1920 and 1923 was attributed to the party's activism, Hitler's dynamic personality, and the ability to attract working class members by using *völkisch* nationalism.[42] Attempts at appealing to workers by using anti-Semitism to argue that Marxism was influenced by Jews, and the use of former Communists and SPD members who had become Nazis, proved to be mostly ineffective. This supports the general national attitude of the German workers, who tended to shy away from anti-Semitism as a reason for joining the Nazi Party.

In the summer of 1922, the Nazis were outlawed in Baden. This banishment proved to be almost unenforceable and contributed to strengthening the position of the party in the area. The local police did little to enforce the ban and the members began to circumvent the law by joining the Munich group.[43] The resurgence of the party in Baden between 1923 and 1933 paralleled the general growth of Nazi power throughout much of Germany. The Baden NSDAP in these years was dominated by urban, white-collar, middle class members between the ages of 23 and 33.[44] In addition, there was a sizable group of artisans, skilled workers, craftsmen, and *Kaufmänner* (professional party activists).[45] For all practical purposes, over three-quarters of the membership in Baden was lower middle class.

The strength of the NSDAP was dependent on a number of interconnecting factors. Early approaches to obtaining power were aggressive, as was evidenced in the *putsch* attempt in Munich in 1923. Popular appeal for such overt acts of militarism and aggressiveness proved to be extremely low. Hitler's *putsch* attempt failed in the short term, but proved to be an important stimulus for the party for the future. While in prison, Hitler refined his ideology and his approach. His written work, *Mein Kampf*, became the source for Nazi ideology and outlined the program for the party's eventual totalitarian leadership role. Hitler also showed flexibility by determining a major change in the party method of obtaining political power. In discussing the failures of the *Bierhalle Putsch* with a friend while in prison, Hitler suggested that a political approach was more viable than force. His new approach was clarified during the conversation when he reflected, "when I resume work, it will be necessary to pursue a new policy. Instead of working to achieve power by armed coup, we shall have to hold our noses and enter the Reichstag against the Catholic and Marxist deputies."[46]

What resulted from this new approach was a blend of politics and terror. The militant SA continued to provide a source of terrorist militancy that could be used to weaken opponents. Hitler also used forms of propaganda that would appeal to large numbers of people without directly committing the party to a specific program.

The NSDAP developed a strong power base by obtaining the support of the rural and small town populace. Nazism became ingrained in an important segment of German society. This foundation made it possible for Hitler's assumption of power in 1933 and the eventual nazification of all of Germany. By the end of the Third Reich, over three-quarters of the population was involved in the Nazi programs, either as active members or as supporters. Some were totally committed to the National Socialist ideology and to Hitler, others were driven into the system due to fear or the possibility of material gain. The NSDAP came to power during a period of national economic disaster. Hitler used the inflation and unemployment to identify the Nazi Party with an opportunity for improvement, albeit while using the most radical means. The Nazi propaganda machine continued feeding the public with the perception that the Nazi era brought the revival of the German economy. What became evident at the end of the regime was that Nazism had so penetrated German society that attempts at totally eliminating the effects were to prove extremely difficult, if not impossible. Through the effective use of propaganda throughout the history of the Nazi Party, a number of the followers continued to carry fond memories of the Third Reich into the postwar period.

NOTES

1. On November 9, 1938, supporters of Hitler's NSDAP attacked Jewish synagogues and businesses, breaking windows, burning buildings, and incarcerating numbers of Jews.

2. Serge Schmemann, "Blunt Bonn Speech on the Hitler Years Prompts a Walkout," *New York Times*, November 11, 1988. The result of this speech was the eventual resignation of Jenninger from the Parliament.

3. "Jenninger Resigns after Kristallnacht Speech," *The Week in Germany*, November 17, 1988, p. 2.

4. Chancellor Kohl reviewed the Nazi pogrom on the anniversary of *kristallnacht* and reminded his countrymen that this event was a source of shame because the majority remained silent, whether from fear or apathy, during the excesses. Throughout Germany, the attempts at remembering these outrages provoked by the Nazis have continued, thereby hopefully diminishing the public stigma. G. Wehomann et al., "Kohl: Kristallnacht a Cause of Shame," *The Week in Germany*, 10 November 1988, p. 1.

5. "Nazi's Computer Games Spreading Propaganda," *Spokane (Wash.) The Spokesman Review*, 3 January 1989, p. 3.

6. Ibid.

7. As recently as February 4, 1989, majority protests against the increasing strength of the newest radical right-wing party, the Republicans, were reported. In West Berlin, protest rallies were conducted by thousands of demonstrators in response to the Republicans, who supported ousting foreigners from Germany, winning 11 seats in the local parliamentary elections. "Germans March in Protest," *Dayton (Ohio) Daily News*, 5 February 1989, sec. A, p. 14.

8. Der Minister des Innern, "Die Herausforderung unseres Demokratischen Rechstaates durch Rechtsextremisten," 1988, 2.

9. Ibid.

10. Franz Josef Strauss died in August 1988, after having spent over 40 years as the head of the CSU.

11. William Shirer, *The Rise and Fall of the Third Reich* (New York: Simon and Schuster, 1960), 44–45.

12. Ibid., 41.

13. Charles B. Flood, *Hitler: The Path to Power* (Boston: Houghton Mifflin Company, 1989), 81.

14. Ibid., 45.

15. Shirer, 42.

16. Ibid., 42.

17. Martin Brozart, *Hitler and the Collapse of Weimar Germany* (New York: Berg Publishers, 1987), 41.

18. Adolf Hitler, *Mein Kampf* (Boston: Houghton Mifflin Company, 1939), 797.

19. Ibid., 798.

20. James D. Forman, *Nazism* (New York: Dell Publishing Company, 1978), 12.

21. Maurice Baumont et al., eds., *The Third Reich* (New York: Praeger Publishers, 1955), 43.

22. Alan Bullock, "The Führer: Portrait of a Dictator," in *Hitler and Nazi Germany*, Robert L. Waite, ed. (New York: Holt, Rinehart and Winston, 1969), 18.

23. William S. Allen, *The Nazi Seizure of Power* (Chicago: Quadrangle Books, 1965), 73.

24. Brozart, 49.

25. Allen, 24.

26. George L. Mosse, ed., *International Fascism* (London: SAGE Publications, 1979), 144.

27. Mosse, 157. George Mosse estimated that the working population made up about 47 percent of the total population. This is supported by Stanley Payne, who argues that the middle class dominated German society in the 1930s. Anyone falling into the categories of white-collar, farmer, self-employed, civil service, and other than blue-collar industry was classified in this definition as middle class.

28. Ibid., 157.

29. Payne, 59–60.

30. Ibid.

31. Brozart, 86.

32. Ibid.

33. Gordon Craig, *Europe since 1815* (New York: Holt, Rinehart and Winston, 1971), 579.

34. Ibid.

35. Mosse, 184.

36. Brozart, 53.

37. Mosse, 184.

38. Ibid.

39. Ibid., 25.

40. Johnpeter Horst Grill, *The Nazi Movement in Baden, 1920–1945* (North Carolina: University of North Carolina Press, 1983), 83.

41. Ibid., 65.

42. Ibid., 55.

43. Ibid., 133–34.

44. Grill, 83.

45. Ibid., 84. The *Kaufmänner* tended to be white-collar employees who floated from job to job or were marginally employed.

46. Craig, 578.

2 The Postwar Years, 1945–1970

The absence of a revolutionary self-purging, of a profound confrontation, of a fundamental political and spiritual catharsis, was to have serious and adverse effects on the political climate of the postwar years. It provided the preconditions of the rebirth of radical anti-democratic nationalistic attitudes and organizations.

Kurt Tauber, *Beyond Eagle and Swastika*, 22

Following World War II, war weariness prevailed throughout Germany. The devastation of the urban centers and the psychological impact of total defeat was an onerous weight on the German population. Shortages of food and fuel made survival the key issue in the minds of the German majority. The Nazis had failed, leaving the populace to face the results of six years of war and to answer for the atrocities committed during Hitler's regime. For all practical purposes, the NSDAP appeared to have disappeared, never to rise again. Hitler's party had combined authority and radical protest to obtain power and then proceeded to crush all opposition.[1] By making themselves as the supreme and only party in Germany, the Nazis touched the entire German society. The populace either submitted to the National Socialists or became victims of the regime; many who refused became inmates at concentration camps or died at the hands of Hitler's SS (Schutzstaffel) or Gestapo.

The defeat of Nazi Germany left the majority who had supported the regime, both actively or passively, in an untenable position. The Allies designated specially trained military units to administer the programs designed to subjugate Germany to the decisions of the victors. The majority of the populace withdrew into a cocoon of passive compliance fearful of how the Allies were going to handle Germany and its population. In cities such as Koblenz, Suhl, and Tuebingen, there were reports that the people were sullen, arrogant, uncooperative, and hostile.[2]

The Allies presumed that Nazism was no longer a viable political force. Many Germans, who had been active members, attempted to hide the relationship, or fled Germany to sanctuaries in the Middle East, North Africa, and South America. However, the majority remained in the Fatherland and eked out a living, dependent on the whims of outside forces, particularly those of the occupation authorities and the Allied leadership.

DENAZIFICATION

Although the Allies immediately began the process of ridding the country of the vestiges of Nazism by developing a denazification program, this proved to be a formidable challenge. The original concept by the United States was to purge the entire U.S. zone of occupation in Germany of all officials who were known Nazi Party members or collaborators. In essence, this entailed firing all of the country's administrators from local through national levels. City and town mayors, councilmen, law enforcement officers, teachers, and other civil servants who carried the stigma of the NSDAP, either directly or indirectly, were relieved of their duties. This caused unusual hardships for local governments, which lost all of the administrative expertise in a time of great need. The devastation of war, the shortage of food and shelter, and the upheaval of the complete German society made this purge all the more traumatic.

One of the first major directives that the Allies incorporated following the war was specifically designed to eliminate the Nazi influences. The Allied Control Council, developed to co-ordinate occupation policy efforts, initiated the Control Council Law Number 2 on 10 October 1945. This law was designed specifically to terminate and liquidate all Nazi organizations.[3] The program resulting from this law became known as "de-nazification." All Nazi institutions, including paramilitary organizations, were made illegal and any attempts at developing a reformed organization that purported to support any Nazi ideology was strictly forbidden. In addition, all property that was considered to have belonged to the NSDAP was confiscated.

Once the occupation authorities were able to begin instituting a postwar policy that was capable of reducing the misery throughout Germany, the denazification efforts were accelerated. By 12 January 1946, the Control Council provided additional guidance for the denazification process. Directive Number 24 began the difficult task of weeding out individual Nazis. This directive explicitly required that Nazis and others who were openly hostile to the Allied purposes be removed from offices and positions of responsibility.[4] This included all people that the Allied authorities deemed to have been more than nominally involved in the Nazis program. The Control Council identified these individuals as those who had held office at the local or national level, those who authorized or participated in Nazi atrocities or discrimination, those who avowed continual belief in Nazism or in racial and militaristic creeds, and those who voluntarily gave substantial moral or material support or political assistance to the NSDAP.[5] In essence, the general nature of this directive placed the onus on the field organizations to determine who did, or did not, meet these criteria. Key to the denazification program was the effort to denazify German industry. The Allies perceived the industrial complex within Germany to be a cornerstone of the Nazi program. Special attention was placed on insuring that industry was totally cleansed of any semblance of National Socialism.

The philosophy behind the widespread approach to rooting out Nazism in industry was clarified in the Control Council directive, which stated that "it is most important to carry out the denazification of industry with the utmost vigor, and the smallness of the enterprise shall be not reason for failure to denazify."[6]

It soon became evident to the occupation authorities that a complete eradication of Nazism was a task that would require tremendous amounts of effort and resources. The United States military estimated that 10 percent of the German population were active as Nazi Party members and an additional "untold millions" had belonged to organizations associated with the NSDAP.[7] The laws and directives supplied by the authorities in Germany were made in almost a political void. Allied leadership, particularly the leadership of the United States, had not provided sufficient policy guidance to the occupation authorities concerning the denazification program. This caused a number of communication problems between the different levels of authority, particularly within the occupied zones. As of late 1946, the president of the United States had not provided a general U.S. policy for occupation.[8] The reason for this shortcoming was an internal dispute within the executive branch of the U.S. government during the latter part of the Roosevelt administration.

After the Teheran Conference in 1943, the European Advisory Commission, the State Department, and the Civil Affairs Section of Eisenhower's headquarters began to focus on the postwar occupation and treatment of Germany. Henry Morgenthau, Roosevelt's secretary of treasury, was not impressed with the plans that would call for a "soft" approach to Germany. Morgenthau argued that a hard line should be taken in dealing with the Germans and that this was the wish of the president. Roosevelt appeared to share Morgenthau's position when he remarked that "we either have to castrate the German people or you have got to treat them in such a manner so they can't just go on reproducing people who want to continue the way they have in the past."[9]

Morgenthau, taking his cue from the president's statement, provided a plan for postwar Germany. He argued that Germany should be reduced to a pastoral economy and that all industry be dismantled. This concept intrigued Roosevelt, who ordered the program initiated, thereby forbidding military authorities from taking action that would strengthen the German economy. The idea was to insure that Germany would not rise economically above its neighbors.

However, an alternative program developed by the triumvirate, consisting of the State Department, the European Advisory Commission, and SHAPE headquarters (Supreme Headquarters Allied Powers Europe), received Henry L. Stimson's support, who was the secretary of war. Stimson argued that it was better for Germany to be gradually rehabilitated industrially and that a central administration be instituted.

As events unfolded in Central Europe, the administration reevaluated U.S. policy in Germany. Morgenthau's program remained in effect for two years, with the United States military modifying the nature of the plan in order to implement the denazification program and meet the requirements of insuring the German economy remained weak.

Supreme Headquarters Allied Expeditionary Force (SHAEF) interpreted the Allied position on denazification in a directive sent to subordinate commands on 24 March 1945. The directive allowed leniency toward Nazis who played minor roles and provided for the temporary retention of Nazis in key positions considered essential for military operations.[10] On the other hand, the U.S. Twelfth Army Group, one of the major subordinate commands, required the removal of all Nazis from all levels of German administration. The U.S. Sixth Army Group followed suit with its sister army group on 30 March 1945, but did allow individuals who had merely affiliated themselves with the Nazis the opportunity to hold minor positions.[11] By mid-April, both army groups standardized their methods of operation with denazification, but remained far more strict in interpretation of the program than SHAEF. The need for SHAEF to adjust to the British and American positions generated the differences. Great Britain felt that a strict denazification of Germany would cause additional problems for the development of an efficient administration. The Americans argued that the president's position under the Morgenthau Plan called for strict methods of denazification, whether it resulted in inefficiency or not.

Even within the areas that the U.S. army groups operated, which were located in central Germany, procedures were not always standardized at the lower levels of occupation authority. Communications of the directives were not always effective, leading to a disparity at the local levels. Plans that the regional districts prepared in order to implement the denazification program were not always provided to the field detachments. These units, in turn, were forced to interpret their requirements without guidance. The differing directives, and the lack of effective communication, caused a situation where different criteria were used throughout the U.S. zone of occupation to identify and disenfranchise suspected Nazis. The result of this haphazard method of dealing with the Nazis was a loss of faith in the denazification program among both the Allies and the German people.

The extent of the denazification in each region was dependent on the local administrators of the program. Interpretation of the directive was key in how these local units proceeded in the denazification of that region or city. A lack of understanding of German psychology, and the undue reliance on the German clergy hindered the total program.[12] The occupation force field teams were often at a disadvantage in dealing with local representatives. In many cases, the difference between a "dangerous" Nazi and the general German public was barely discernible. It became difficult for the officers assigned to identify the dangerous Nazi, or to tell the difference between active and less active support for the regime. The question of why the Germans supported such a regime continued to linger in the minds of the investigators. The difficult decisions over an individual's guilt were often predicated upon that person's participation in supportive roles. This gray area blurred the individual's actual involvement in the atrocities associated with the NSDAP.

An inspection team that was responsible for evaluating the effects of the program provided interesting insights into the different standards that were being practiced in the American zone. In a letter dated 6 July 1945, which was prepared following a visit by a member of this team to a number of field detachments in central Germany, Lieutenant Colonel Mitchell Wolfson, SHAEF, stated that "in general the detachments are not doing a thorough job of denazification. It becomes apparent that it requires a great deal more work, effort, and tough-mindedness than are now being exercised by most detachments."[13]

Under the requirements placed on the U.S. forces, the field units experienced a tremendous drain on their resources and capabilities because of denazification. A survey conducted at the end of June 1945 showed that out of 216 respondent field detachments, only 20 had finished denazification in their locales.[14] It was also found that a good number of these organizations decided to use individuals who were proven Nazis in critical administration positions until suitable replacements could be found. This was, of course, in contravention to the army groups' directive for denazification and showed the inability of the local organizations to follow the guidance in accordance with perceived presidential wishes. The result of this survey was an increased effort throughout the summer of 1945, and upon the dissolution of the Anglo-American command (SHAEF), the extension of stricter denazification requirements, which included not only government, but German culture and economic institutions.[15]

Being placed into the tenuous position of deciding who would, and would not be ostracized, the denazification officials tended to rely heavily on the local clergy. These clergymen, many of whom could have been considered tainted for actively supporting the Nazis, often recommended the appointment of administrators to resolve local issues, knowing full well that these same officials had tainted pasts.

These inconsistencies and lack of effective guidance resulted in a public uproar.[16] The media in the United States provided graphic detail about the ex-Nazis being placed in official positions and the inability of the occupation authorities to stamp out Nazism.[17] The condemnation through the press further weakened the effect and efforts of the denazification program.

The sheer weight of the requirement to root out all Nazis was overwhelming. Thousands of dossiers on suspected Nazis became backlogged as teams attempted to ascertain whether these individuals met the criteria for legal charges or discharge from specific duties.

Meanwhile, the need for trained administrators to provide

leadership throughout Germany was becoming acute. Numerous officials who were considered qualified were also identified as Nazi supporters. This was due to the fact that nazification had been far more complete at the higher levels of German administration. The void left by denazification was not sufficiently filled to provide the basic leadership needed to overcome the postwar trauma and nation-building requirements at the local level.

The president and Morgenthau construed the portion of Stimson's plan dealing with Nazi administrators as being too easy on the Nazis.[18] The Allied Control Council was caught in a difficult position, not knowing what methods to follow. Therefore, they hedged on their specific policies that were supposed to be followed by the field organizations. However, the winter and spring of 1946–47 brought on an economic crisis and increased tensions with the Soviets, who emphasized the dismantling of German industry over humanitarian interests. This led to a revised "level-of-industry" plan that authorized the German industry to increase their capacities to 70 to 75 percent of their 1946 levels. This, in effect, repudiated the purpose of the Morgenthau Plan and allowed the Stimson Plan to gain popularity.

Criticism of the methods used, and the apparent inefficiency of the denazification system, led the U.S. occupation authorities to turn the program over to the Germans on 5 March 1946, only one year after the initiation. This placed the occupation authorities into a role of direction and supervision, but allowed the Germans the opportunity, with their greater resources, to proceed with the denazification process.

The Germans initiated their program by passing the "Law for the Liberation from National Socialism and Militarism." This law was designed to adjust the procedures in order to curtail the more ardent protests against the denazification program. In essence, the law rejected the previous methods of using summary procedures to identify Nazis, which had been based on the concept of collective guilt. Identification of individuals was predicated on individual responsibility and accountability. The new law allowed an individual the right to respond to allegations made against him, or her, and the law recognized different degrees of culpability.

The Germans soon became acutely aware of the difficulties associated with a denazification program. Even with the changes in procedures as outlined in the new law, which resulted in a number of those dismissed under the U.S. system being reinstated, the shear size of the project became overwhelming. A new personal questionnaire was required of all Germans in order to determine prior Nazi affiliations. Approximately 13 million individuals turned in these questionnaires within the U.S. zone.[19] Of the respondents, roughly 75 percent were deemed as not chargeable under the law. The remaining 25 percent, totalling approximately 3 million were required to be subjected to an oral trial-like interrogation that was designed to determine culpability. This number was more than the German legal system could effectively manage. Therefore, the standards were lowered, showing a tendency for increased leniency.

By August 1946, the "Youth Amnesty" was passed that allowed all people born after 1919 to be granted amnesty from denazification procedures. This was followed six months later, in February 1947, by the "Christian Amnesty." These pardons were given to all individuals deemed materially underprivileged or disabled. Both of these amnesty programs were specifically designed to lessen the judicial backlog associated with denazification.

The changing procedures were indicative of changes occurring in postwar Germany, particularly as Western relations cooled with the Soviet Union. U.S. policy in Germany began to change dramatically in the early fall of 1946. Secretary of State James F. Byrnes, in a speech in Stuttgart on 6 September 1946, provided an insight into this changing policy. His comments suggested an end to the "occupation's punitive phase."[20] On 12 March 1947 the Truman Doctrine was incorporated into U.S. foreign policy. This presidential declaration said that the United States was joining in a global commitment against Communism.[21] This deepened the Cold War between the Western Allies and the Soviets. The Western Allied zones merged in February 1948 because of continued friction with the Soviets and a need to strengthen Germany's economic base. This also guaranteed West German inclusion into the European Recovery Program. These two actions were designed to begin grooming West Germany as a future Western ally as the lines between East and West began to solidify. The United States showed more leniency in regards to the denazification program as Germany was drawn into the Allied fold.

The dichotomy existing between the need for a denazification program and the need to restructure a severely damaged society that could effectively support the Western Alliance led to a domestic crisis within postwar Germany. By 1949 it was apparent that denazification was not a viable method of dealing with the severe problems of reconstruction. In November 1949 the occupation authorities reneged on Directive Number 24 and Law Number 2. A new law was passed that provided amnesty and civil rights to former members and followers of the Nazi Party and former *Wehrmacht* officers.[22] In response to queries over the reasons for this unprecedented action, the Allies touted the German efforts to develop a sound democratic order and the achievements of Germany in rebuilding.[23] Ex-Nazis were granted the right to vote and the right to stand for election. *Wehrmacht* officers were allowed to enter public service, commerce, or the professions. The caveat was that those who were Nazi activists, or war criminals, were excluded from this amnesty.

The result of this amnesty proved to be important in the continuation of National Socialism. The lesser Nazis were released and they proceeded to reenter German society on an equal basis with their countrymen. In addition, a large number of major participants in the NSDAP were released. Alfred Krupp was an excellent example. The owner of the Krupp Steel Works, this industrial giant was an active supporter of the Nazis and provided invaluable service to the Nazi war machine. Following the war, Alfred Krupp was found guilty of utilizing slave labor in his company. For this, he was sentenced to twelve years in prison. Krupp served only three years of the sentence and upon his release was reinstated as the head of the revitalized Krupp Steel Works.[24]

As the Germans made denazification more lenient and the United States became less strident in pursuing ex-Nazis, those individuals who had been active Nazis, often in positions of importance, found a way to circumvent the system. Usually these people had sufficient time and resources to wait for the denazification program to lose much of its impact. With the continued lessening of importance placed on denazification, these ex-Nazis began to resurface and reenter the mainstream of German society. SS Lieutenant General Georg Schreyer and SA Chief of Staff Wilhelm Schepmann took advantage of the leniency.[25] Both of these highly placed Nazis were granted a category V classification, which classified those incriminated by the law but who received dispensation because they had presumably actively resisted the Nazi regime. By obtaining this category it allowed them the opportunity to reenter the West German employment force.

The reintroduction of past Nazis into the German society in 1949 provided an opportunity for the continuation of Nazi sympathies. Many of the released ex-Nazis resumed the radical nationalist activities that they were forced to abandon in 1945.[26] These activities were closeted in "legal" political parties which remained on the right-wing fringes of the Federal Republic's political circle.

The effects of the denazification program were far-reaching. The U.S. military in Europe spent a disproportionate amount of time over a four-year period attempting to effectively support the program. The results stirred wide controversy, causing the greatest perplexity among allies and providing material for widespread media coverage in the United States.[27] The excesses of denazification, and the haphazard procedures used, discredited the entire effort in the minds of the majority of the Germans. This discredit created a situation that the postwar Nazis could use to further their efforts to gain back a semblance of political power.[28]

The only other Allied postwar policy that caused as much, or more, controversy than denazification involved the Nuremburg trials of those Nazis charged with crimes against mankind. Public opinion of both policies was often mixed. What is certain is that the denazification program was so extensive in scope that it was doomed to be unsuccessful. The unsuccessful elimination of Nazism opened the doors for the continuation of an ideology that had caused unheard of atrocities in modern times and which carried a potent antidemocratic philosophy that continued to fester on the right-wing fringes of German society for over 45 years.

THE RISE OF RIGHT-WING POLITICAL PARTIES

The inability of the Allied occupation authorities and the new German government to totally denazify Germany led to a reestablishment of right-wing interests during the early post-war years. The remnants of Nazism were able to survive because of the ineffectiveness of the denazification program and the policy differences that continued to be instituted by the separate occupation zone authorities. In the U.S. zone, the decision to authorize ex-Nazis to once again participate in the political sphere prompted many of the old party faithful to reestablish right-wing connections. Nazi sympathizers continued to exist, as evidenced by the gatherings of ex-SS members and numerous clandestine meetings held during the 1950s and 1960s. Newsletters were distributed throughout the 1950s that provided common information sources for many of the old-time Nazi sympathizers.[29]

Most of these meetings and connections were kept conspicuously quiet in order to remain unimportant in the eyes of the Allies and the new German government. Opinion polls taken in the late 1940s suggested that right-wing interests still existed, although only a very few groups were considered radical. A study of German public opinion conducted in the U.S. zone of occupation during the years 1945 to 1949 presented some interesting statistics. The study concluded that roughly 15 to 18 percent of the adult population in the immediate postwar period were unreconstructed Nazis.[30] What is important is that the 15 percent figure approximates the estimates of potentially extreme nationalists that continue to surface from 1945 to 1968.[31] By 1953, in interviews conducted by the *Institut für Demoskopie* (Institute for Opinion Research), approximately 5 percent of the West German population supported the idea of a resurgence of the Nazi Party.[32] Although a 1956 interview showed only 3 percent still supported this view, the fact remained that a portion of the population was carrying forward the Nazi ideology over ten years after the defeat of Nazism. These statistics show a general decline of "hard-core" support. However, there were a small number of people who advocated either all, or part, of the ideology.

This small minority of the population provided a base for the influx of rightist political organizations that developed in the postwar period. As had occurred in the years of the Weimar Republic, a number of right-wing factions that represented the broad spectrum of rightist sympathies from moderate to radical began to evolve in postwar Germany. Control of the emerging nationalist parties was contested between the original conservative nationalist leaders and the radical nationalists, who maintained Nazi sympathies.[33]

Within the atmosphere of nationalist resurgence was a growing distinction between the generations of Nazis. On the one hand there were those who had been politically involved with the *Freikorps* (Free Corps), constituting a good number of the early right-wing factions and those who had been within the Weimar military structure. Many of these individuals became the first Nazis, many of whom had adjusted their individual ideologies to parallel the ideology of the NSDAP. These Nazi supporters joined the movement in the 1920s and then survived the many changes within the party. On the other hand, there were those individuals who were totally trained within the NSDAP. These people included those who were subjected to the intensive propaganda programs associated with the Hitler Youth, the SS (*Schutzstaffel*), and the internal organs of the Nazi Party. These trained cadres tended to become members of the Nazi Party after the party took control of Germany, therefore distinguishing themselves from the early members who had fought the battles to place the NSDAP into the position of the dominant political force within Germany.

These two groups of ex-Nazis set the stage for the evolution of right-wing parties in postwar Germany. The conflicts in methods and ideology were instrumental in the inability of the

Table 2.1
German Extremist Right-Wing Parties, 1945–1959

1945-1952	1953-1959
1945 2 parties	1953 14 parties
1946 1 party	1954 16 parties
1947 2 parties	1955 11 parties
1948 4 parties	1956 11 parties
1949 6 parties	1957 8 parties
1950 11 parties	1958 8 parties
1951 12 parties	1959 7 parties
1952 74 parties	

Source: Hans-Helmuth Knütter, Ideologien des Rechtsradikalismus im Nachkriegsdeutschland (Bonn, 1961), p. 31. Note: The selection of these parties was predicated upon the government definition of right-wing extremism. This definition suggested that parties that were formed, or had substantial membership, from those with Nazi background, or had neo-Nazi leanings, were then considered right-wing extremists.

early parties to coalesce into an effective right-wing movement. Until 1949, the ultra-Right placed its efforts toward the organization of mass parties that could compete with the Social Democrats (SPD) and the Christian Democrats (CDU). These early efforts were often squelched by the occupation authorities, who saw these nationalist efforts as a potential reversion to the days of the NSDAP. After 1949, the nationalist right wing began to set up clandestine networks of leadership which eventually provided the political expertise to organize an effective right-wing political party.[34]

The largely ineffective efforts by the old Nazis to produce a viable political party in the late 1940s can be attributed to the results of World War II. The war brought war weariness, questions of Nazi atrocities, and a deep sense of defeat. The nationalist movement after the war was unable to overcome these factors, which insured that no unified, politicized, and radicalized war generation was available that could be energized to support a resurgence of the nationalist fervor.

The first decade following the war became the period of steady increases in the number of rightist extremist parties. These parties, however, tended to split each year. The numbers of active supporters remained low in comparison to the total population. As Table 2.1 indicates, the number of parties increased steadily from 1946 to 1951. In 1952, the number of parties jumped to 74, primarily because of the splintering of the Socialist Reich Party (SRP) following the government ban of the party. By 1953, the number of parties restabilized as many of the splinter groups either combined or were outlawed by the government. Interest in the extremist parties began to diminish in 1957 and continued to attract little attention, or interest, through 1959. The average estimated membership of these early parties was 35,000.[35]

Other sources claim that the 1945 membership in these radical groups was 18,000 and by 1959 the membership numbers had increased to 56,200.[36] These estimates support the average estimate previously noted, but also provide a sense of slow growth in the nationalist support base.

It is important to note that the continuation of right-wing radical interests was not expunged following the war and that a small, but active fringe remained to attract nationalist minded individuals. The majority of these early parties stayed within the bounds of legality during the first decades after the war. Those that did not were quickly banned by the occupation zone authorities or the Federal Republic government. However, the banning of these radical political groups did not dissolve the support that had been obtained. These banned organizations resurfaced under new organizational names, but with modified platforms and often the same leaders.

A number of other types of rightist organizations flourished during the late 1940s. Most of these groups included political associations and youth groups that supported conservative platforms, which were well within the bounds of German law. Over a ten-year period, approximately 400 parties, groups, and associations were identified within the western zones.[37] There were those, however, which specifically tended to attract the extremists. These radical right-wingers were normally the products of the Nazi movement. Having been exonerated by the Allied postwar policies, many of the SS veterans and those reared in the *Hitlerjugend* (Hitler Youth) formulated political organizations that often went beyond the limits of the West German constitution and laws.

The precursor for many of the later right-wing extremist

parties was the Socialist Reich Party (SRP). This particular organization was founded in 1949 by intellectuals who initially lost their positions and opportunities during the denazification program.[38] Many of these individuals were striving for a return of their self-respect and a semblance of security and influence, much of which was lost during the denazification process.

The Socialist Reich Party was founded on principles dedicated to the eradication of both the internal and external political order of the postwar Germany.[39] The party became more extremist each year. Ultimately, the government branded the SRP as being the direct successor of the Nazi Party.

The overall West German population in 1949 was broken into three major economic categories. Over 50 percent of the population was centered around agriculture, with approximately 20 percent involved in industry and another 10 percent in commerce and transportation.[40]

The SRP membership was fairly evenly distributed between these general categories. Thirty-two percent of the membership was estimated to be involved in agriculture, 35 percent in commerce and transportation, and another 33 percent were considered entrepreneurs.[41]

Many of the heavy industrial areas provided support for the right-wing SRP. In these areas, the blue-collar membership was dominate, but there were adequate representatives from both white-collar groups and intellectuals.

In the southern areas of Germany, particularly in the states of Baden and Württemberg, the majority of SRP members were involved in commercial occupations, free-lance professions, and public administration.[42] These differences indicated a support base in the South that was skewed toward the white collar and commerce.

The membership proved to be multi-societal and expelled the idea that only the unemployed and farmers subscribed to right-wing extremism. One major similarity dominating the membership was common religious interest. Almost without exception, members of the Protestant faiths dominated the chapters of the SRP throughout West Germany from 1949 to 1952.[43]

There was more interest in the SRP in northern German regions than in the south. For example, by 1951, the states of

North Rhineland and Westphalia accounted for 1,300 active SRP members.[44] In the far northern states of Schleswig and Holstein there were 700 to 800 members.[45] However, in the more southern states of Baden and Württenberg, the estimates were much lower, at approximately 400 members.[46] In Bavaria the membership was less than 200.[47] Although the party insisted during this period that membership exceeded 30,000 to 40,000 members, most observers argue that the membership more accurately totalled 10,000 persons throughout West Germany.

The Socialist Reich Party did make some political progress during their short history. In the 1950 national elections, the SRP was able to receive 11 percent of the vote in its first appearance in a major election process. These early results brought the SRP to the attention of the Allied authorities and the Federal Republic government.

The SRP attempted to strengthen the position of the right wing by merging with other groups. Two key organizations that were approached were the growing National Democratic Party of Germany (NPD) and the National Reich Party (NRP). An initial merger attempt was made in 1950, but was unsuccessful due to a continuing conflict between leaders. The inability of these right-wing organizations to fuse was the same problem that has been habitually the nemesis of the right-wing movements throughout Europe and in North America. The rightist ideology of a strong centralized authoritarian type of government provided the basis for continued fracturing. The inability of each separate organization to subordinate to another left the right wing in an exposed and divided position.

The Socialist Reich Party eventually disintegrated because of negative publicity and its inability to obtain support of other right-wing groups. On 23 October 1952, the West German courts outlawed the SRP by enforcing laws that were promulgated at the end of the war to protect the constitution against usurpation. The judicial findings against the party included the increase in radicalism within the SRP, the promotion of Hitler era methods of obtaining publicity, and the use of the election position of 11 percent to pressure the government.[48]

Many of the members of the SRP foresaw the eventual out-

come of the judicial proceedings against the party and began
to move their activities underground as early as autumn 1951.
A number of new organizations were developed, increasing
the right-wing factionalism fivefold in one year. By 1953, many
of these groups had folded or were merged with other
organizations.

The leaders of the SRP attempted to reinstate the party as
a new political entity by changing the name. This effort failed.
The German judicial system issued the verdict that "it is
forbidden to substitute organizations for the SRP or to continue
existing organizations as substitute organizations."[49] This allowed the growing NPD (*Nationaldemokratische Partei
Deutschland*) to gain the dominate position as the premier
right-wing party in Germany.

Not all Germans accepted the banning of the SRP graciously.
Although the general consensus of the population was that the
SRP was, in fact, the successor of the old Nazi Party, a poll
taken among the West Germans in January 1952 showed a
strong empathy for the Socialist Reich Party. Only 23 percent
of those polled support the ban.[50] In contrast, 43 percent favored
banning the Communists, who were considered far more dangerous for the new German democracy.[51] Thirty-two percent
were against banning the SRP.[52] Whether the 32 percent supported the SRP directly, or indirectly, or whether these people
felt that the ban was exceptional punishment is difficult to
ascertain. The fear of losing individual rights and freedoms
may have been important in the responses. The large numbers
of people who opposed the banning were, more than likely, not
convinced that a party which had obtained 11 percent in a
major election could be considered as dangerous as judged by
the government.

The result of the ban was the elimination of a growing
extremist right-wing power base that showed early success in
West German politics. The party's tendency to become more
radical and to bring back memories of Hitler's regime proved
to be the SRP's downfall. Those who supported this right-wing
party moved into other groups or joined underground extremist
movements that remained relatively quiet for over two decades.

Another smaller right-wing party, the DRP (*Deutsche*

Reichspartei), emerged in 1946. This party was the primary ultra-conservative organization in lower Saxony until 1964, at which time the DRP and the NPD merged. In 1953, the DRP won 1.1 percent of the votes in the Federal Parliament.[53] This initial political showing proved that ultra-conservative rightist feelings still existed in this region of Germany. By 1953, this political power base had received 3.8 percent of the popular vote in the lower Saxony state elections.[54] Later, in the 1950s, the Rhineland Palatinate provided the DRP with additional fertile grounds for political strength. The ultra-conservatives garnered a surprising 5.1 percent of the votes during elections in the Rhineland Palatinate in 1959.[55] Over the following five years, the DRP's political strength waned in lower Saxony, which dropped to 1.5 percent of the popular vote in 1963, and in the Rhineland Palatinate, which dropped to 3.2 percent of the votes.[56]

The interim period between 1946 and 1964 was a cyclical period for the DRP. As was so often the case with other right-wing groups, the DRP was hampered by a splitting within its ranks. The moderates, led by Hermann Klingspor, were unable to overcome the increasing power of the radicals within the party. Klingspor proved to be a weak leader, who tended to miss meetings and therefore was unable to control events. Whenever negotiations were begun between the radicals and moderates, Klingspor was often unavailable or would leave the negotiations. This provided the opportunity for the radical members to gain the majority control of the DRP. The ultimate result was a failure on the part of the moderates to develop a viable rightist political bloc and obliterated any chances of developing a rapport with the Bonn government.

In 1946, the British gave permission for the DRP, along with another conservative party, the German Conservative Party (DKP), to participate in the political process. By August 1949 these two parties made a reasonable showing in the elections. Combined, the DKP and DRP within the British zone of occupation received 430,000 votes.[57] The DKP obtained 118,000 votes in the North Rhinelands and Westphalia, whereas the DRP accounted for 273,000 votes in lower Saxony, their traditional early stronghold.[58]

The period between 1949 and 1964 was a difficult time for the DRP. The radicals in the party perceived the reintroduction of a parliamentary system in Germany as an attempt to return the Weimar method of government. The fear of another weak republic hardened the radical position against the efforts of the moderates to cooperate with Bonn.

In the German state of Hesse, the NPD under the leadership of Heinrich Leuchtgens, made early attempts to merge the DRP with the NPD. The reason for the merger attempt was to try and control the radical elements in each party. The moderates in the two parties thereby hoped to retain the overall control of the electorate.[59] Although an agreement was reached in September 1949, the whole merger process almost broke down when the radicals within the DRP, led by Dr. Walter Kniggendorf, alias Walter Bergmann, attempted to thwart the joining of the two parties.[60] Following the ratification of the merger in Hesse in 1950, Kniggendorf was expelled from the DRP and subsequently joined the SRP as the party propaganda chief.

By 1951, the DRP was losing a good number of the nationalist votes to the Socialist Reich Party. The National Reich Party and the DRP tried to develop a coalition to return the right-wing votes to their candidates. The outcome was a continued infighting among the two major party's leaders and within the parties themselves. In comparison to the 1949 votes that the DRP had received (430,000), in 1953 the party only obtained 296,000 votes.[61] The greatest losses that the DRP experienced were in their own stronghold of lower Saxony, where over 50 percent of the membership abandoned the party in 1953. In Schleswig-Holstein, the DRP also experienced over a 50 percent drop in support.

A key right-wing party that provided a home to many ex-Nazis and ultra-right supporters was the *Nationaldemokratische Partei Deutschland* (NPD). Founded officially in the mid-1940s by Heinrich Leuchtgens, the NPD championed the right-wing conservative views for over 35 years. This party developed in central Germany and proved to be the most resilient of the far-right parties. Originally designed to uphold conservative opinions, the party began to woo old Nazis in April 1948 as the denazification program declined.

As was the case with other right-wing parties, the NPD was forced to deal with an ideological split within its organization throughout its existence. Carl Heinz, a strong advocate of Nazi-oriented ideology and ex-Waffen SS member, split from Leuchtgens in early 1948.[62] In December 1949, radical right-wing members in the party under the leadership of Karl-Heinz Priester, a past member of the Hitler Youth and protégé of Carl Heinz, broke from the NPD. Priester continued to use the NPD name, but began the extremist radical faction. These continual cases of radicals breaking from the main party tended to weaken the NPD over the three decades following its initial organization. After having enjoyed success in elections in the 1960s, the party's decline to a fringe position in the 1970s spelled defeat for the moderate elements within the organization. By the early 1980s, the German majority and the Bonn government considered the NPD as an extremist right-wing party.

In addition to the growth of right-wing political parties was the continuation of the traditional German military bond. Veteran groups were once again activated, providing the ex-soldier a sense of comradeship as the years diminished their numbers. One of these, the Waffen SS veteran's organization, provided an opportunity for many of the ex-Nazis to retain acquaintances and to insure a visible military-oriented association to postwar generations. Both directly, and indirectly, this organization insured that the military of the Third Reich was recognized by the younger Germans. They directly supported youth groups and political parties with similar interests. Indirectly, they reminded the population of Hitler's SS, which included the ceremony and camaraderie that was inherent in these groups. Many of the young people, who became active in the neo-Nazi organizations of the later 1970s and 1980s, fashioned their militaristic themes after those of the Nazis, particularly the SS. The use of uniforms, banners, and utilization of a variation of the SS symbol (⚡⚡) were indicative of the return of many of the outward appearances of the NSDAP.

The key to the small—approximately 25,200 members in 1987—yet active right-wing extremist movement, is the dichotomy between a rabidly antiright-wing extremist stance taken by both the moderate conservatives and the liberals presently active in West German politics and the continuum of right-wing sympathies that remained quietly on the fringes of the political system since the end of World War II.

Nationalist tendencies were still apparent in the NPD party throughout the 1960s and 1970s. Albeit this was a very small party of less than 38,700 members at its peak political strength in 1967, which was unable to obtain the minimum 5 percent of the popular vote that would make it a viable political party. The largest conservative parties, the CDU (*Christian Demokratische Union Partei*) and the CSU (*Christian Sozialistische Union Partei*) of Bavaria also provided an opportunity for nurturing of the right-wing tendencies on their far-right fringes. Although moderate conservative parties, they did offer a political party environment in which right-wing extremists could continue to develop a following.

GERMAN DEMOCRACY AND THE RIGHT WING

The emergence of extremist right-wing parties in the postwar period can be attributed to a number of events that occurred during the era of reconstruction. However, although these events provided opportunities to the right-wing extremists, the results were subject to the strengths and weaknesses of the politicians that formulated the new Federal Republic government. Each West German leader detracted or enhanced the opportunities of the right wing simply by the emphasis placed on suppressing the radical Right.

Konrad Adenauer, the first postwar West German chancellor, proved to be a formidable opponent to the right-wing interests in the immediate period following the establishment of the new Federal Republic of Germany. His early efforts resulted in strengthening the West German government as a viable Western democracy and he was largely responsible for the economic upturn within Germany. These changes forced the rightist political parties, particularly the NPD, to reevaluate their approaches to the electorate. No longer could the Right effectively use the argument that the Allied occupation of Germany was a hinderance to economic development. There-fore, in order to maintain a position of political strength, the Right began to use problems dealing with reunification, re-armament, and neutrality as keys to their platforms. They questioned the viability of the North Atlantic Treaty Organi-zation (NATO) as a method for maintaining peace in compar-ison to the possibilities of Germany remaining neutral. Reunification was favored over the formation of a Western Eu-ropean community. Using these arguments, the extremist right-wing parties were able to attract a small base of support throughout Germany during the 1960s as the Cold War intensified.

Adenauer's years in power severely limited the effects of the right wing. A majority of the conservative vote was obtained by the Christian Democrats (CDU) and the *Deutsche Partei* (DP). The loss of popularity experienced by the radical right was the result of the rapid recovery of the German economy, Adenauer's strong anti-Communist stance, and the strength-ening of the European Common Market.

With the retirement of Adenauer in January 1963, the NPD began to gain strength and was vying to become a potential right-wing political power. The late 1960s were the best years for the party. However, during this period the NPD was accused of being neo-Nazi in leadership and in ideology. In fact, 12 of the 18 members of the party directorate were accused of having been active Nazis.[63]

Adenauer's replacement, Ludwig Erhard, became embroiled in intra-party feuds, thereby losing much of his political strength. A good number of the Christian Democrats began to fear the possibility of a potential failure of the Federal Repub-lic, similar to that experienced with the Weimar Republic. In order to survive, coalitions were forged between the Christian Democrats who were traditionally conservative, and the Social Democrats who leaned toward the left. This alliance provided the Social Democrats the opportunity to gain a position within the government for the first time since before the war.

In addition to Adenauer's retirement and the realignment of the political power within the government, there were the con-tinuing political arguments that provided impetus for a right-wing revival. Of constant concern for many Germans was the question of reunification. The building of the Berlin Wall was a prime indicator that reunification was becoming a more distant possibility. Adenauer's inability to preclude the building of the wall and a disintegrating relationship with East Germany provided grist for the right-wing arguments. The NPD was a strong supporter of reunification throughout the 1950s and 1960s, which drew support from the postwar population.

The NPD's support for increased efforts in reunification was tied to other interests that were important to the West German populace in the 1960s. The fear that Germany was headed for a severe economic recession, and the fact that NATO appeared to be placing Germany in a tenuous position with the East, were issues that the NPD used to gain popular support. German neutrality became a key issue for the nationalist organizations.

The NPD collected votes from a large number of small businessmen and farmers by using the argument that the Federal Republic of Germany was sliding toward a weakened position reminiscent of the Weimar days. Tied to these arguments, the party moved away from anti-Semitism in order to insure that they were within the limits of the law, and began to vocalize against the *Gastarbeiter* (foreign guest worker). In addition, a strong voice was raised against the continuing "Americanization" that was turning Germany into an Americanized community. As nationalists, the NPD argued that it was essential to retain German heritage and to eliminate the growing U.S. influence that was permeating the entire German society. Finally, the NPD wanted the return of discipline and order that was slipping away with the apparent weakness at the governmental levels.

Membership in the National Democratic Party during the peak of the organization of the mid-1960s was indicative of the growing neo-Nazi interest throughout Germany. The directorate for the party in 1964 and 1965 was made up of 45 percent prior DRP members, 55 percent National Socialists that had joined the Nazi Party after 1933, and 17 percent who were "old" National Socialists and had been Nazis prior to Hitler's seizure of power in 1933.[64] These modern nationalists supported a modified nationalist ideology that was designed to provide a strong foundation for a rebuilding of Germany. Inherent in this governmental and societal remake of Germany was the basic philosophy that the "new" society must be built on a "hierarchical elitist structure which incorporates undemocratic management that insures that conflicts are eliminated."[65]

The NPD, therefore, became the focal point for the rising neo-Nazi interests in Germany. The late 1960s provided a window of opportunity for the neo-Nazis to again develop a power base. The leadership and a sizeable number of the party membership had lived during Hitler's era and were therefore imbued with the NSDAP ideology. Younger people became attracted to the NPD through contact with these older ex-Nazis and the semi-clandestine nature of the movements surrounding this reemergence of ultra-right influence. As the party influence began to disintegrate in the early 1970s, these radical elements became more pronounced in the movement toward extremism.

Estimates of membership showed a decline from a high of 56,200 members in the NPD in 1959 to a low of 20,700 in 1964.[66] From 1965 (26,300 members) through 1967 (38,700 members), the party began a period of steady, but modest growth, which resulted in the winning of a number of local elections.[67] These years correlated with a general economic downturn, albeit not a major recession, that caused concern among the working class. As the German economy began to rebound in the late 1960s, the membership again plummeted, falling below the 5 percent (4.3 percent) mark in 1969. The right-wing radicals were dependent on an economic decline to gain support throughout the 1960s and into the 1970s. The result was a failure of the NPD to develop a viable political base and almost total disintegration of the party in the early 1980s. The extremists within the NPD and other right-wing parties became disenchanted with the lack of political opportunities for the right and moved toward affiliation with more militant groups that were often outside of the law.

Although there were a large number of right-wing organizations during the era from 1946 to 1970, the most radical, such as the banned SRP, the DRP, and the NPD, provided the haven for right-wing extremists. In 1964, German Minister of Interior Hermann Hoecherl estimated that there were 112 extremist right-wing organizations in Germany with a total membership of 27,000.[68] In addition, there were an estimated 46 newspapers and periodicals with a circulation of approximately 200,000 that were published by these right-wing groups.[69] These figures are indicative of extremism that remained on the fringes of German society in the 1960s. In 1965, the Ministry of Interior warned of an increase in right-wing extremism and suggested that the membership, circulation of newspapers, and acts of terrorism by this far-right radicalism had tripled.[70]

Studies conducted by the government in the 1950s and 1960s showed that parties identified as neo-Nazi were predominantly male oriented and were favored by male voters.[71] The women voters appeared to tolerate the neo-Nazi groups, but tended to vote conservatively with the more moderate conservative parties, such as the CDU and CSU.[72]

The neo-Nazis of the 1960s were generally described as men with only grade school educations, two to six years of military service, and between 35 and 50 of age.[73] Those who showed the most nationalistic tendencies were often farmers, followed by men with more than six years of military service. The third category of militant nationalists came from the ranks of the intellectuals, particularly those who had university degrees.

Early signs of the right-wing radicals use of terror were evident in the 1960s. In March 1963, a 21-year-old student, Hans Juergen Bischoff, was killed while preparing a homemade bomb in his home in West Berlin. Bischoff was, at the time of the accident, a member of the radical right-wing group, "The National Students League." The German government had become sensitive to a growing fear of right-wing terrorism. The police believed that the "League," or *Bund*, was involved in 16 explosions along the Berlin Wall, as well as a bombing of a Soviet tourist travel agency.[74] Government officials saw the similarity of these bombings to those perpetrated by the Nazis against frontiers set up by the Versailles Treaty.[75]

For the most part, these early attempts by right-wing radicals to use terrorist actions were limited. The government considered these acts as isolated incidents of criminal action by individuals or small groups of extremists, but not a major threat to the nation.

The political parties on the Right preferred to stay within the boundaries of legality. Those who did not, for example the SRP, were dealt with quickly. Right-wing nationalists provided the leadership for a number of the parties. Many of these leaders had continued to maintain strong Nazi affiliations. Terrorism was not the common practice in the formative years of the parties due to the valid attempts to use a political course to gain power. The right-wing political base suffered in periods of economic growth, whereas the government seemed to wax stronger.

THE RIGHT WING AND GERMAN YOUTH

James Forman, in his book *Nazism*, argued that the twentieth-century movements, particularly those associated with the Nazis, were rooted in nineteenth-century romanticism.[76] The training of the German youth was a key element in the methodology employed by Hitler. By providing a party foundation of youth, the NSDAP was assured the potential of the continuation of the Third Reich. A total immersion of the young Germans into Nazi ideology set the stage for a program of leadership that was designed to continue the evolution of the Nazi power. In essence, this foundation provided the extremist right wing with the postwar leadership of many of their youth organizations.

The defeat of the National Socialists brought about the dissolution of the Nazi era youth organizations. Although these groups, generically referred to here as the *Hitlerjugend* (Hitler Youth) and the *Bundesmädchen Deutschland* (League of German Girls)[77] were organizationally dissolved, the concepts and ideology were more difficult to eliminate. Many of these young people knew only the Nazi philosophy and methods. Naturally, many of those who had taken these lessons to heart were still amenable to retaining extremist right-wing tendencies during the postwar years. In essence, the Hitler Youth provided the opportunity for the growth of similar manifestations of an organized rightist youth following the war.[78]

The right wing became evident in the youth organizations and political parties as the political opportunities expanded in postwar Germany. A vast number of groups, as many as 140 different youth leagues, sprang up over the 20 years following the war.[79] Many came into being and were dissolved shortly thereafter, due to inadequate support or splitting. Most of the groups ranged from moderate rightist to short of radical. A few became militant and carried on many of the traditions exemplified in the Hitler Youth of the past. These groups are the ones that became associated with neo-Nazism during the late 1970s and early 1980s.

Kurt Tauber, in *Beyond Eagle and Swastika*, provided an extensive evaluation of right-wing groups that evolved between 1945 and 1965. He categorized the youth organizations into groups ranging from those that leaned toward the *völkish* historical traditions of German nationalism to those who were associated with right-wing political parties.

Tauber referred to the first group as *Bündisch*. The organizations that fall into this category supported the traditional *völkish* nationalism similar to that of the early Hitler Youth. The primary emphasis of these organizations was the desire to restore a linkage with the past, particularly the traditional German *völkish* past.[80] These types of youth groups were unable to capture a good following after the war.

On the other hand, Tauber identified the non-*Bündisch* youth as the most promising source of youth support for the militant right wing during the period. This category, divided into *völkish* groups and military-patriotic groups, did reasonably well during the period of 1945 to 1965. Using regimentation, order, and authority, the leadership attracted young recruits.[81] The *völkish* groups were fashioned after the nationalist organizations that sprang up during the Weimar republic. The military-patriotic organizations were generated by adult associations and political parties.

An excellent example of a youth group developed by a political association was the *Jugendkorps Scharnhorst*. This organization, founded in 1952, was supported by the postwar

Stahlhelm, a group that had roots in prewar Germany.[82] The *Jugendkorps Scharnhorst* tended to be fairly radical and militant and used surprisingly similar methods employed by the prewar *Stahlhelm*.

Another radical organization that dominated the far-right youth groups in the 1950s was referred to as the *"Kyffhäuser* Youth."* These young people were organized in 1954 and included participants from ten different *Länder* (states) within West Germany. By 1956, the *Kyffhäuser* group had merged with a number of other right-wing organizations into the much larger *Deutscher Jugendbund Kyffhäuser*. The leaders of this reorganized group were Herbert Schmidt of Dortmund, and Karl Klauka of Cologne.

The sheer numbers of these youth groups and the large active membership dominated the conservative youth movements of the 1950s. By the 1960s, the numbers of nationalist-oriented youths had dropped considerably, which was evidenced by a major decline in identifiable youth organizations. The greatest number of overt right-wing youth activities throughout the 1960s and early 1970s were sponsored by the conservative political parties. These sponsorships provided the parties with young party recruits and developed a base for the future of the party.

There are a number of estimates of membership populations in youth groups that were known to exist during the 1950s and 1960s. A former Hitler Youth member turned journalist, Günter Welter estimated that there were 40,000 to 70,000 youth that belonged to extreme right-wing youth groups in 1960.[83] The student journal, *Civis*, in a late 1960 article, supported Welter's higher estimates by saying that youth membership in the radical right was close to 70,000.[84] This number included all young people associated with right-wing groups, both political and social and with extremist leanings.

On the other hand, the Federal Republic government argued that the number of members during the early 1960s was only 3,000.[85] This lower estimate suggests that the standards used for identifying "radical" youth members were not the same among estimators. The government only counted those youth that were specifically identified as neo-Nazi or who showed a tendency to be militant. It appears that the definition of an extremist right-wing youth was not clarified, thereby allowing the journalists, demographers, historians, and the government to interpret the radical membership from their own perspectives. Other studies seem to support the higher estimates and therefore tend to look at the extremist youth similarly to the nongovernment studies. Tauber supports the estimates of the demographer, Arno Klönne, who suggests that the most probable number of extremist youth during this period was in the range of 40,000.[86] In support of Klönne's figure, Tauber included those of Nikolaus J. Ryschkowsky, who in his studies *Gesellschaft zum Studium Zeitfragen* and *Studien von Zeitfragen*, argued that the most realistic figure would be between 25,000 and 30,000.[87]

These estimates of membership are difficult to correlate, simply because of the lack of information concerning criteria used to distinguish who was considered "extreme." In most cases, the estimates used included both West German and Austrian neo-Nazi groups. No delineation was made between the members as far as citizenship. It would appear, however, that the government's estimate of 3,000 was either totally predicated on "dangerous" elements in the extremist groups or the government was uninformed as to the extent of the right-wing influences among the German youth. The estimates of 30,000 to 40,000 activists in right-wing militant groups is probably a better indication of the extent of the membership in these organizations during the late 1950s and early 1960s. These figures were supported by a return evaluation in 1962, when the newly estimated numbers correlated to the earlier ones. This later study excluded the more moderate youth groups such as the *Junge Adler* (Young Eagles) and the *Deutscher Pfadfinderbund* (German Scout League).[88]

The Germans traditionally organized their youth into special interest groups. In 1961, 38 percent of the Federal Republic of Germany's youth was organized.[89] This means that approximately 4.5 million young people belonged to some kind of organized club or society. Of this number, an estimated 1 percent were organized into nationalist groups, indicating that approximately 45,000 youth were involved in rightist groups.[90]

A number of studies were conducted that attempted to identify the reasons that the majority of the German postwar youth shied away from radical movements. Within the university student population, Jürgen Habermas et al., in their work *Student und Politik*, provided some of the criteria for the student positions.[91] Habermas and his fellow researchers studied student activities at the University of Frankfurt. The conclusions drawn showed a distinct lack of identification between the students and the Bonn government. These students showed no understanding nor interest of the democratic political system and often were negative toward politics in general. This study suggested that the key to disinterest on the part of the majority of these college-oriented youth involving political movements was that these students possessed "emotional attributes" that are psychologically associated with a "democratic personality structure."[92] This psychological structure inhibited the tendencies of the subjects from supporting mass organizations such as those that dominated the prewar youth. What is important about this study is that the general membership in right-wing groups did not come from the university environment, but tended to come from the working class, rural regions, and technically trained. These young people traditionally felt the effects of recession first and were the most vulnerable to outside influences. But even within this group, the interest in supporting a mass movement, such as neo-Nazism, was limited.

Those who espoused the nationalist ideology, although in a minority, were also studied. The results indicated that these particular youth shared many identifiable characteristics. A sense of solidarity within the family is a key element for a good portion of these youth members. Many children felt that their fathers were persecuted for being patriotic and for remaining loyal to the German (Nazi) government. Therefore, some of these same children inherited the resentments that were associated with the parents and relatives who felt betrayed or unfairly condemned following the war.

Other youths became members of nationalist organizations in an attempt to rebel against their parents or the establishment. This rebellion was not necessarily limited to the right-wing membership, but was an important determinate for young people to join either the right-wing or left-wing organizations in the 1960s.

In addition to the familial relationships that drove the younger generation to radicalism, the educational system played a role as well. Schools, which traditionally provide the foundation for future opinions and practices, were under a tremendous disadvantage in postwar Germany. The West German schools during the 1960s were staffed by teachers who were often trained during the Nazi period. An estimated 50 percent of the teachers, teaching in the mid-1960s, were trained under the auspices of the Nazi Party program.[93] In addition, the rules governing postwar schools in Germany required that the curriculums of these institutions were to be devoid of all references to the Third Reich. In essence, this led to a generation of German youth who graduated from secondary schools and who were often naive to politics and unable, therefore, to evaluate the German past. This inability to correlate the Nazi past with the postwar political environment led many young people to assume that nationalism was important to German sovereignty and German identification.

MILITANT YOUTH

The organization of youth groups continued throughout the 1950s and 1960s. Most of these groups were designed to attract young Germans who wanted to enjoy the same interests in hobbies, sports, or politics. The political parties throughout West Germany developed and nurtured a number of youth organizations. These youth organizations that were supported by the conservative and radical political parties were important in providing future recruits for the party membership.

The more extremist right-wing political parties supported the militant youth groups. This was especially true in the case of the *Reichsjugend*, a youth organization led by Walter Matthaei. This group was organized under the auspices of the SRP, but was unable to extend its activities due to the Bonn government's efforts to eliminate the SRP in the early 1950s. This particular youth organization attracted a number of radical young people and supported a number of goals that were reminiscent of those of the NSDAP. The SRP used the *Reichsjugend* movement to provide support for the party activities. Included in the duties given the youth group were responsibilities associated with propaganda work and the guarding of local rallies held by the party. In addition, the members of the youth organization provided a volunteer labor service that was designed to accomplish local tasks and bring the membership together in a common cause relationship.

After the banning of the SRP, the rise of the NPD provided the impetus for additional youth organizations. A number of groups were linked to the NPD over the past 40 years. Those that were the most militant and became identified as neo-Nazi included such organizations as the "Young Storm Troopers," "The Young Vikings," and "The Ring of Youth."[94] All of these groups were linked either directly or indirectly to the National Democratic Party. The members of these particular youth organizations wore brown shirts, black knickerbockers, peaked hats, and buckled belts.[95] At their meetings and at their parades, these militant youth used military march music and were disciplined according to the Hitler Youth Book, *The Steel Hat Handbook* (1927 edition).[96] The leaders of these militant NPD youth groups were the former SS officers, Dr. Karl Ganser and Karl Lehmann-Teja. Both of these men epitomized the most militant right-wing extremists in postwar Germany.

The radical elements within the NPD provided the leadership for other youth groups. Although not considered as militant as the aforementioned youth organizations, the numbers of more moderate groups mushroomed in the 1950s and 1960s. Examples of these youth organizations included groups such as the *Nationale Jugendgemeinschaft* (National Youth Fellowship), organized by a suspected NPD member, Hans Schulz. This organization was predicated on a program that was against the "liberal west-oriented Adenauer government."[97] In addition to the specific right-wing groups with more extremist programs, there existed other youth organizations that were more moderate, but yet were definitely conservative along right-wing lines. A number of *Bündische* (associated) nationalist youth groups supported anti-Communist activities and the rearmament of Germany. Other groups, referred to as non-

bündische nationalists by Kurt Tauber, tended to argue against the Federal Republic's army, the *Bundeswehr*, and the Western occupation and involvement within West Germany. These groups felt that the *Bundeswehr* was an embarrassment to German military capabilities and it appeared to be emasculated by the constitutional requirement for limiting the forces to less than 500,000. The British continued use of the term "occupation forces" when referring to the British presence in West Germany, together with the dominance of U.S. forces, rankled many of the younger German nationalists. Other youth organizations often supported the basic German laws, but were guided by the interpretations of those laws as presented by the veterans groups and the right-wing political parties.[98]

A vast number of young people did belong to different youth organizations during this period. However, a majority were not interested in the options available through the right-wing political groups. Those that did become active members of nationalist groups tended to lean toward the more moderate organizations. There were a few who, reminiscent of the past Hitler Youth, became active in those far-right militant groups that continued supporting past Nazi virtues and ideology.

The NPD was never able to easily attract young people. The leaders of the party attempted to prove that the party was well within the bounds of the legal German democracy. These attempts were generally ineffective in providing a base in which the majority of young Germans could identify. On the other hand, many of the more militant radical youth were alienated by these attempts at moderating the party platform to comply with the laws dealing with the preservation of the constitution. This caused many of these extremists to drift to the far-right neo-Nazi groups.

What was apparent in observing the leadership of many of these radical youth groups was the preponderance of ex-Nazi leaders. Many of the leaders had been active NSDAP members, or SA and SS members.[99] Both the SRP and the NPD were heavily influenced by members and leadership that had been actively involved in the Nazi regime. The youth groups associated with these right-wing parties were brought into direct contact with these "older" party functionaries. The more militant youth groups were influenced by these men who carried the past into the relationship. The ex-Nazis and SS members offered a sense of past glory and carried forward the need to remember the positive aspects of the Hitler Youth programs and the military traditions of the Third Reich.

For the most part, the extremist activities of these youth groups were kept in check during the first three decades following the war. This was a period of relative calm, although the Nazi ideology remained active among the more radical groups.[100] There were isolated incidents that the government construed to be individual acts, or localized acts, and perpetrated by individuals associated with right-wing youth groups. In December 1959, the city of Cologne was faced with a case of anti-Semitism. Swastikas were painted on various Jewish cultural sites, which led to a number of minor anti-Semitic incidents by a group of young DRP members.[101] These incidents were quickly resolved by the city officials and the individuals involved were punished without a great amount of publicity. The incident was determined to be an isolated case where a very misguided youth had stepped over the boundary of good taste. This situation was not considered to have been promulgated by any type of major youth movement, nor did it appear to receive general support among the majority of young people in Germany. It is interesting to note that although a number of youth groups did exist during the 1950s and 1960s, many of which contained radical elements, the importance of these groups to the general public was considered negligible. When considering the actual estimates of the numbers of active extremists, and the fairly clandestine programs they participated in, this view can be understood. On 6 January 1960, the Ministry of Interior estimated that 15 to 18 radical youth groups existed, and that there were "only" 2,300 members.[102] This number represented the most extreme neo-Nazi activists. The Ministry of Interior refined the estimate in an article, *"Für die Demokratie,"* in which the author stated that there were 15 right-wing radical groups with as many as 2,950 members and an additional five militaristic groups with membership as high as 2,750.[103]

Although the numbers of right-wing radicals appeared to be

minimal in comparison to the overall population, the fact that such groups existed and were often led by ex-Nazis, showed that a foundation of youthful extremists continued to survive in the postwar period. These radicals provided the opportunity for the growth of more militant neo-Nazi organizations, many of which became more openly active in the 1980s, both on the European Continent and in the Western Hemisphere.

NOTES

1. Peter Shipley, "Patterns of Protest in Western Europe," *Conflict Studies* 189 (1988), 6.

2. Joseph R. Starr, *Denazification, Occupation and Control of Germany, March–July 1945* (Salisbury, NC: Documentary Publications, 1977), 19.

3. Control Council, Allied Occupation Forces, U.S. Zone, West Germany, *Official Gazette* 1 (29 October 1945), 19.

4. Control Council, *Official Gazette* 5 (31 March 1946), 98.

5. Ibid.

6. Beate Ruhm von Oppen, *Documents of Germany Under Occupation, 1945–1954* (London: Oxford University Press, 1955), 103.

7. Kurt B. Tauber, *Beyond Eagle and Swastika* (Connecticut: Wesleyan University, 1967), 28.

8. Harold Zink, "The American Denazification Program in Germany," *Journal of Central European Affairs* 6 (October 1946), 228.

9. Frank Freidel, *Roosevelt: A Rendezvous with Destiny* (Boston: Little, Brown and Company, 1990), 530.

10. Zink, 228.

11. Ibid.

12. Ibid., 230.

13. Starr, 130.

14. Ibid., 131.

15. Ibid., 132.

16. Zink, 231–32.

17. A good example of this situation occurred in Aachen, a city on the German-Dutch border. The U.S. field team went to the local clergy and asked for recommendations for a city administrator. The individual recommended was placed in charge. Soon after the appointment, it was brought to the attention of the field team that this particular individual had been a Nazi official. The publicity over this

particular situation was extensive in the United States and led to a continuing debasement of the entire denazification program.

18. Zink, 228.

19. Tauber, 30.

20. Tauber, 35.

21. The Truman Doctrine was presented to Congress as a needed commitment to the growing Communist threat, which appeared to be worldwide. The Soviet Union's consolidation of power in Eastern Europe and their attempt at control in Iran provided the Truman administration the opportunity to develop Cold War stance. Economic aid to Greece and Turkey offered the best option to take a hard stand against Communism. Truman used the Greek civil war as the reason for offering economic and moral support for anti-Communist efforts, which resulted in a declaration of U.S. foreign policy that was dedicated to the blocking of Communism around the world.

22. von Oppen, 436.

23. Ibid.

24. John Ardagh, *Germany and the Germans* (New York: Harper and Row, 1987), 390.

25. Tauber, 33.

26. Tauber, 82.

27. Zink, 227.

28. Tauber, 36.

29. Walter Laqueur, *Germany Today* (Boston: Little, Brown, 1985), 150.

30. Abraham Ashkenasi, *Modern German Nationalism* (Cambridge, MA: Schenkman Publishing Co., 1976), 59.

31. Ibid.

32. Christopher Emmet and Norbert Muhlen, *The Vanishing Swastika* (Chicago: Henry Regenery Co., 1961), 9.

33. Tauber, 80.

34. Ibid.

35. Hans-Helmuth Knütter, *Ideologien des Rechtsradikalismus im Nachkriegsdeutschland* (Bonn: Ludwig Röhrscheid Verlag, 1961), 32.

36. Ashkenasi, 109.

37. Tauber, 982.

38. Ibid.

39. Ibid., 709.

40. Ibid., 699.

41. Ibid.

42. Ibid.

43. Ibid.

44. Ibid., 697.

45. Ibid.

46. Ibid.

47. Ibid.

48. Tauber, 714.

49. *Das Urteil des Bundesverfassungsgerichts vom 23. Oktober 1952, betriffend Feststellung der Verfassungswidrigkeit der Sozialistischen Reichspartei* (concerning the constitutionality of the Socialist Reich Party), published by members of the *Bundesverfassungsgericht* (Tübingen, 1952), 5.

50. Ashkenasi, 63–64.

51. Ibid.

52. Ibid.

53. Peter Janke, *Guerilla and Terrorist Organizations: A World Directory and Bibliography* (New York: Macmillan, 1983), 15–16.

54. Ibid.

55. Ibid.

56. Janke, 16.

57. Tauber, 727.

58. Ibid.

59. Ibid., 729.

60. Dr. Kniggendorf joined the Nazi Party in 1927 and became an SS officer. He worked as a functionary within Goebbel's Propaganda Ministry and was an official of the *fölkish*, anti-Christian religious movement. Although Kniggendorf carried the title of Ph.D., he was found to have fraudulently appropriated the title. In investigations conducted, it was found that he had never received the Ph.D. from the University of Göttingen.

61. Tauber, 805.

62. *Die Neue Zeitung* (Munich), 29 April 1948.

63. John Ardagh, *Germany and the Germans* (New York: Harper and Row, 1987), 395.

64. Ashkenasi, 107.

65. Ibid., 92.

66. Ashkenasi, 109.

67. Ibid.

68. Dennis Eisenberg. *The Re-emergence of Fascism* (New York: A. S. Barnes and Company, 1967), 201.

69. Ibid.

70. Ibid., 211.

71. Ashkenasi, 64.

72. Ibid.

73. Ibid., 64–65.

74. Eisenberg, 194.

75. Ibid.

76. James D. Forman, *Nazism* (New York: Dell Publishing Co., 1978), 12–13.

77. The *Hitlerjugend* and *Bundesmädchen Deutschland* were themselves subdivided into groups according to age.

78. Tauber, 385.

79. Ibid., 982.

80. Tauber, 397.

81. Tauber, 427.

82. The *Stahlhelm*, prior to the war, was an association of World War I veterans that battled the Weimar republic under the assumption that the government had betrayed the German soldier by accepting the Versailles Treaty. The postwar group, although only a shadow of its prewar strength (10,000 in comparison to 1,000,000), called on front-line soldiers without regard to class, religion, or party affiliation, to stop the subversive forces endangering the German peace, order, and security. By 1952, the *Stahlhelm* had become increasingly radical. Field Marshal Albert Kesselring, upon his release from prison, assumed the role of the organization's president. His efforts to bring the radicals and the moderates of the organization together were largely unsuccessful. A new position was taken which said that the group was no longer a fighting organization. However, the importance of insuring that the members and the youth were trained in soldierly attributes became a major goal. The "new" approach also supported the concept that war was a destroyer of values, opposed Marxism, and supported the EDC Treaty. A large number of members were unwilling to accept these more moderate goals, resulting in continued fracturing within the organization.

83. Tauber, 366.

84. Ibid.

85. Ibid.

86. Tauber, 366.

87. Ibid.

88. Tauber, 367.

89. Ibid., 370.

90. Ibid.

91. Ibid., 381.

92. Ibid.

93. Tauber, 431.

94. Eisenberg, 198.

95. Ibid.

96. Ibid.

97. Tauber, 416.

98. Ibid.

99. Knütter, 34.

100. Although one would think that the relationship between the right-wing and the rising left-wing phenomenon in the 1960s would have been less than congenial, strange liaisons were found to have occurred. In the mid-1960s, the Baader-Meinhof group, a left-wing terrorist organization, had a need for weapons. A known underworld type, Hans Jürgen Bäcker, recommended a most unusual source for these weapons. He suggested that the group contact a secret cadre of the NPD, known as a neo-Nazi organization. Two members of the Baader-Meinhof group, Astrid Proll and Irene Goergens (the former an escapee from a state home and the latter an illegitimate child of a U.S. soldier), went to a Charlottenburg bar, *Wolfschanze*, and met with Günter Voigt, a member of the neo-Nazi group, who sold the leftists a Beretta handgun and 250 rounds of ammunition for 1,000 Deutschmark. Jillian Becker, *Hitler's Children* (Philadelphia: J. P. Lippincott, 1977), 102.

101. Ashkenasi, 132.

102. Knütter, 34.

103. Ibid.

3   Survival of the Fittest

> As long as we [Germans] still encounter tremendous gaps in the
> historic thinking of many of the younger citizens about the in-
> sanity of the National Socialist regime, there is a need to use
> every occasion to deepen at least our basic awareness.
>
> *The Week in Germany*, 10 November 1988

The 1970s and 1980s were years in which the right-wing extremists drifted away from established parties, such as the CDU/
CSU and the NPD, and joined clandestine radical groups. These
organizations were the most militant of the right wing, which
the government referred to as neo-Nazi. The leadership within
many of the rightist groups also changed during this period.
Those ex-Nazis who were influential in the right-wing political
movements throughout the 1950s and 1960s were slowly replaced by a new generation of younger Germans through normal attrition. The new leaders began to synthesize old Nazi
ideas with newer ideologies, most of which applied to the postwar changes in Germany. These revised ideologies included an
anti-foreigner position, particularly against the Turks, which
was similar to the anti-Semitism of the past. Members of the
Besitzbürgertum and *Bildungsbürgertum*, the propertied and
academic bourgeoisie, provided support and empathy to this
rising group of right-wing politicians and activists.[1] Many of

these wealthier and educated Germans assumed the role of saviors of German conservatism. Numerous right-wing tracts of literature appeared that were supported by gatherings of the authors and their interested readers. The upper middle class property owners supplied a sense of respectability to a movement dominated by the lower middle class.

The postwar generations did not identify with the problems associated with the war years. Rapid industrialization made Germany a European economic power in a short period of time. Old Nazi chichés, which played on the economic woes of Germany and on the unfairness of the postwar treaties, were no longer viable. The new generation within West Germany was attuned to a portion of Germany that was once again an important central European industrial region. On the other hand, they were aware of the division of Germany and the potential threat that existed from the Soviet bloc of Eastern Europe.

Although this new generation was, for the most part, not inclined to support the old Nazi methods, there was still a semblance of the "old" party ways and ideology that crept into the emerging right-wing political platforms of the late 1970s and early 1980s. The influence of the ex-Nazis, although diminishing with age of the members, was still apparent in many of the political positions taken by the major right-wing parties.

The majority of the right-wing political organizations incorporated the concept of a strong central German nationalism within their platforms. This was used to support the idea that law and order, as well as strong government, were the best methods of governing the German state. The dream of a unified Reich continued to provide a rallying point for Rightist interests. Right-wing adherents identified this Reich as a centralized German state that would be powerful enough to dominate central Europe. The ultimate German state would be one in which individual interests were subordinated to a common and firm authority of a strong government.

As was the case with the Nazis, the new right-wing activists of the 1970s supported the belief that it was essential for German society to maintain German social values. This was the basis for the position taken against the increasing immigration of foreigners into West Germany. Immigration of foreigners provided an important rallying point for many Germans in the mid-1980s and increased the political power of the right-wing extremists.

The new generation of right-wing supporters and their leaders still believed in the conservative suspicions against personal mobility and expressions of individuality.[2] These suspicions were directed against the apparent liberalism of the Bonn government and provided a growing sense that German society had become far too liberal-oriented throughout the 1960s.

An increased interest in socialism within West Germany occurred during the 1960s resulting in more left-wing support, particularly among those of the upper middle class who had pursued higher educational training. Membership in the radical leftist groups, such as the Baader-Meinhof gang, was composed of the young intellectuals. The conservative traditions of German society appeared to have been thrown aside for the liberal standards, which the right-wingers viewed as being far too loose and ineffective.

Once again, the right wing appeared to be a viable political option for the lower middle class. These were the people in German society who normally leaned on the traditional German values of hard work and orderliness in their daily lives. Many found the liberalism of the 1960s antithetical. This attitude provided fertile grounds for right-wing political recruitment of support from those of lesser social background from the rural and small town environments.[3]

A growing number of members of the petit bourgeoisie began to obtain the primary positions of importance throughout the right-wing organizations. In many cases, these new faces replaced the long dominant ex-Nazis who were active in the NPD and the more militant neo-Nazi groups. In other situations, the two groups worked together providing a common front against the rise of liberal influences, such as the government positions on immigration, social programs, and human rights versus law and order.

Although right-wing leadership changes occurred during the 1970s, the inflexibility of the right-wing ideology made it difficult for the membership to continue supporting ideas carried forward from the Nazi past. Time had dimmed the memories of the prewar generation and the postwar generation was unable to come to grips with a past that was unpopular among the majority of West Germans. The inability for many of the members to accept the past made adjustment to the Nazi era, and the subsequent acceptance of the moral responsibilities of the Third Reich, extremely difficult.[4]

The right wing began to weaken politically during the early 1970s. The German population as a whole appeared less inclined to accept a nationalist program, primarily because of the bad memories associated with war. Therefore, the philosophical arguments inherent in the nationalist traditions were ineffective among the German majority. However, this did not preclude the continuation of a fringe right-wing political effort that continued throughout the 1970s and into the 1980s. This point was clearly shown when a Munich institute was commissioned by the German chancellor's office in 1979 to study the influence of the right wing on German society. The results of the study concluded that the right-wing problem "was more serious than had been supposed."[5]

Although the radicals and extremists of the right wing had existed on the fringes of German society since the end of the war, the majority of the German population and the government had tolerated or ignored these groups. For the most part, this tolerance was predicated on the fact that these radical factions consisted of small numbers of members, many of whom were aging. In view of the fact that the majority of radicals appeared to be prewar Nazis, it was hoped by many West Germans that the eventual loss of these old Nazis from the right-wing organizations, due to age, would ultimately force the extremists to wither away naturally.

The late 1970s, as evidenced by the study performed by the Munich Institute, proved that this thesis was wrong. Although the aged leaders were dying, or retiring, a resurgence in membership of ideologically sustaining extremists continued. The neo-Nazis began to develop a more substantive following under such leaders as Michael Kühnen, who was in his early twenties and a former *Bundeswehr* lieutenant. Loose associations developed between a number of neo-Nazi groups and Kühnen's newly organized *Aktionsfront Nationaler Sozialisten,* which shared ideas and gave mutual support. Members were predominantly under the age of 30 and were the most extreme activists that had been associated with the Right since the 1920s. In 1978 and 1979, these neo-Nazis began a series of attacks and robberies in the Hamburg and Bergen-Hohne regions that were designed to build a financial foundation and which netted approximately 150,000 Deutschmark.[6] In addition, in the investigations that resulted from these robberies, it was found that Kühnen's group had planned an attempt to free Rudolf Hess, an imprisoned Nazi "war criminal," and also to mount an attack on the Berlin Wall.[7]

These incidents of militancy awakened the German government to the increasing activity of neo-Nazi groups throughout Germany. No longer was it politically feasible to overlook the right-wing extremism that had smoldered below the surfaces of rightist politics for over 25 years following World War II.

RIGHT-WING EXTREMIST POLITICS IN THE 1970s AND 1980s

The *Nationaldemokratische Partei Deutschland,* more commonly referred to as the NPD, had been the traditional right-wing stalwart in German politics since 1952, following the prohibition of the pro-Nazi SRP. But after the partial successes of the 1960s, the NPD went through a major decline in popularity in the 1970s. The party's zenith during the 1960s proved to be a weak expression of support by the German electorate against the economic recession that dominated this period. As the German economy strengthened in the early 1970s, the influence of the right wing, and in particular the NPD, began a downward trend in popular support. This trend brought the party to near extinction in the late 1970s and early 1980s.

The only West German states in which the NPD showed a propensity to survive during the difficult decade of the 1970s were Baden-Württemburg and Bavaria. Within these particular areas the protestant enclaves provided some minor, but indicative, support for the NPD through a small membership and a fairly inactive leadership. However, the party remained generally exhausted of strength and was unable to obtain the necessary votes to win seats in any of the local political administrations.

The 1980s began an era of increased right-wing activity throughout Germany. A move toward a more flexible platform by the conservative party, the Christian Democrat Union (CDU), prompted the leader of the sister conservative party of Bavaria (CSU), Franz Josef Strauss, to comment on the eventual results of a conservative move toward the center in German politics. He stated that a move of the conservative parties of Germany toward the center "would open the right to the increasingly active extremist nationalist groups."[8] His worries appeared to be prescient as the almost defunct NPD began a small but timely comeback in elections beginning in 1986. The October 1986 elections resulted in a tripling of the NPD votes in the national elections as the right-wing candidates received a total of 0.6 percent of the popular vote.[9]

The primary reasons for the strengthening of the right-wing support were twofold. A number of these votes were received from the agricultural regions in which agricultural subsidies were greatly reduced in the early 1980s. The second major impetus was the support of the right-wing position against foreigners, which included occupation forces, asylum seekers, and work immigrants. A growing resentment against foreigners, especially against workers and political refugees from Turkey, provided a common rallying point for many of the lower middle class. This particular part of German society perceived a growing threat to their future employment opportunities as the foreign worker assumed many of the more menial jobs throughout Germany.

A coalition of the major right-wing political entities strengthened the increased rightist political activity that was developing during the mid-1980s. Although the NPD had stagnated during the 1970s and early 1980s, the slack was taken up by the quickly growing *National Freiheitliche* (National Independents) right-wing groups. The *National Freiheitliche* coalition was organized and led by Dr. Gerhard Frey, a 54-year-old rightist with a history of supporting anti-asylum legislation against foreigners and for providing a conduit of support for obtaining the release of Rudolf Hess from prison.

By 1986, the *National Freiheitliche* movement had acquired a membership of 12,000. Only one year later that number had risen to 15,100 members. This then made the NF the largest right-wing party in West Germany. On 5 March 1987, Dr. Frey supported an initiative to found a new extremist right-wing party by combining the emasculated NPD with the portions of the largest segment within the NF called the *Deutsche Volksunion* (DVU). The new coalition was brought under the leadership of Dr. Frey and was named the *Deutsche Volksunion-Liste Deutschland* (DVU-Liste D). Although a number of members of both the NPD and the DVU did not join this new organization, there were enough (estimated at around 6,000 in 1987 by Dr. Frey) to provide a strong central core for political action. The DVU remained the largest right-wing union with over 12,000 members, but lost the leadership of Dr. Frey, who had provided the personal contacts and energies that had increased the membership so radically during the mid-1980s. Frey's contacts with Austrian and Tyrolian nationalists, as well as the French right-wing extremist group *Front National* (FN), led by Jean Marie Le Pen, had been important in insuring the DVU an international appearance of psychological and moral support. With the organizing of the DVU-Liste D coalition, these contacts were assumed by the new party structure. By combining elements of the DVU and NPD, Frey was able to organize an extremist right-wing force that was capable of drawing support from the larger DVU party and the small, but still active, NPD.

The 1986 election results were a harbinger of the coming 1988 and 1989 elections. A perceived need for a conservative and nationalist approach to the apparent foreign "threat" drew an ever growing number of voters, although still only a minute portion of the population, toward the right-wing parties. A voter restlessness over Helmut Köhl's leadership was epitomized in the spring of 1988 as the fringe parties on the Right in Baden-Württemburg gained 5 percent of the popular vote and the traditional conservative party, the Christian Democratic Union (CSU) dropped from the 52 percent of four years earlier to 49 percent.[10] The fringe parties that enjoyed the greatest increases included the NPD and the DVU-Liste D, which saw an increase from 1 percent of the popular vote in 1987 to 2.1 percent in the 1988 elections.[11]

This doubling of the right-wing vote in Baden-Württemburg began a resurgence of the NPD and developed a growing political base for the CVU-Liste D at the expense of the traditional CDU. In retrospect, the gains of the NPD during the spring of 1988 were made in rural and economically depressed districts of the Baden and Württemburg regions. Southern Württemburg, in particular the district of Biberach, provided 3.1 percent of its popular vote to the right-wing NPD. Hohenlohe, located in northern Württemburg, showed a 3.6 percent support rate for the rightist candidates.[12] The traditional CDU strongholds in the Black Forest region, located in the southwest corner of West Germany, provided the largest increases in NPD support. The district of Calev, in the northern part of the Black Forest region, provided 3.9 percent of the popular vote to the right-wing party. The southern Black Forest region had results of 3.9 percent in Rottweil, 4.6 percent in Tuttlingen-Donauschingen, and 4.9 percent in Villingen-Schwenningen.[13] All of these results were indicative of a growing concern in this part of Germany that the CDU was not meeting the needs of the German ultra-conservatives. Such topics as intra-German policy, abortion, women's rights, the right of asylum, and a growing dissatisfaction with the government's agriculture policy led to a split within the nation's conservative voting base. The moderate conservatives in the CDU/CSU veered away from the hard-line approach, attempting to temper their positions in order to gain the moderate and centrist votes. Strauss's fears appeared to have been valid. Germany's small Jewish community voiced these same fears through newly elected leadership in the late 1980s. The West German Jewish community responded to the election results with a distinct concern for the potential of a revival of neo-Nazism.[14]

By early 1989, the right wing began to show an even stronger popular support. The 1989 city election results in West Berlin, held in early February, provided the first indication of a substantial right-wing revival. The *Republikaner* Party (REP), a fairly new organization with leanings toward the right, led by an ex-Waffen SS member, Franz Schönhuber, garnered enough votes in West Berlin to capture 11 seats in the local parliament.

The REP was an offshoot of the CSU Party of Bavaria. The party was formed in 1983 by two dissidents who had left the CSU, Franz Handlos and Ekkehard Voigt. By 1985 the party had begun to attract a number of conservatives who felt that the existing traditional conservative parties were unable to provide adequate support for the more rightist positions.

Franz Schönhuber was attracted to the Republican Party in the mid-1980s. Schönhuber had spent the years following the war drifting from one political party to another. He had supported the NSDAP in the 1930s and 1940s. Following the end of the war, he then joined the SPD, the German party that was traditionally supportive of socialist programs and which was antithetical to the ultra-rightist ideologies of Nazism. After a short stint with the SPD, Schönhuber then moved to the conservative CSU. By the mid–1980s, he had returned to the far Right and had become the spokesman for the new Republican Party.

As the primary spokesman for the REP, Schönhuber argued that the party was not extremist or pro-Nazi. In an interview with *Der Spiegel*, a popular German magazine, he said that "the Republicans are good people . . . whose members are police, border guards, soldiers, and civil servants."[15] Schönhuber vehemently argued that the Republicans were only right of middle and that those who suggested that they were extremists, because of the REP position taken in regards to foreigners, would have to say that "there were then extremists with the CDU-CSU."[16]

A number of German newspapers supported Schönhuber's contention that the Republicans were not extremists. An article placed in the *General Anzeiger* (Bonn), following the West Berlin elections, argued that the Republican Party was not neo-Nazi.[17] In supporting this position, the article outlined the platform on which the Republicans obtained the increased popular vote. This platform included the repeal of the right of parole for violent criminals, support of life sentences for drug dealers, a stand against election rights of foreigners, and support the use of the Swiss program of foreign worker rotation.[18] The *New York Times* interpreted the main points of the Republican Party platform to be the ejection of asylum seekers that have been denied asylum in Germany, life imprisonment for drug dealers, and job parity for Germans.[19] These less than extremist yet conservative positions, doubled with the fear that a number of ex-Nazis were associated with the REP, led to the SPD labelling the Republican Party as right-wing extremist.[20] The SPD also claimed that the Republicans had contacts with the NPD and the *Deutsche Volksunion* (DVU), both of which are generally considered to be the most radical of right-wing parties. The fear that the REP was another extremist right-wing party led to a general outcry against the party's gain within the political arena. Following the February elections in West Berlin, demonstrations against the Republicans occurred in West Berlin and in the Bavarian region, where the center of the Republican Party power was located. An attempt by the REP to meet in Nüremberg in late January 1989 resulted in a demonstration in which six people were injured, four of whom were policemen, and "numerous beer glasses and other bar paraphernalia were thrown about."[21]

The actual position that the Republican Party maintains on the Right is difficult to ascertain. What became apparent over the past five years is that many within the West German population, although still only a fairly small minority, have begun supporting more conservative approaches to modern German problems, particularly in dealing with foreigners. The crystallization of a more conservative approach to dealing with recent political and social developments has provided the opportunity for the more extreme right-wing organizations, the political parties and those on the fringe of German law, to develop a much wider potential source of membership.

However, the reaction of many of the Germans to the increasing political power demonstrated by the right-wing parties has shown that the majority still consider radicalism and extremism as unacceptable methods for making political change. The West Berlin elections provided a beginning for the

Republicans, but indicated a willingness on the part of a minority to believe that the REP is still a moderate right-of-center organization that can provide a semblance of conservatism. Much of the West Berlin population reacted to the REP winnings with rage and demonstrations were conducted throughout the city. However, the negative response of a good number of West Berliners did not displace the fact that the right wing obtained approximately 7.5 percent of the local votes and assumed 11 seats in the local parliament.

Throughout 1989 and into 1990, the argument persisted among the majority parties of West Germany about the true interests of the Republican Party. Was this party a neo-Nazi organization hidden behind a veil of legal conservatism? Or was the REP a legitimate political party that supported truly conservative interests that were reflected in the changing German climate of unification, economic adjustment, and limited resources?

Gerhard Boeden, president of the Federal Office for the Protection of the Constitution, replied to journalist inquiries in the spring of 1989 that the *Republikaners* "are on the extreme fringe of the democratic spectrum and thus are not far removed from the threshold to extremism."[22] What became quite apparent during the most recent growth period of the Republican Party was the number of participants who had direct links with the NPD. This tainting of the "new" party by members who were known to have been directly associated with the most extreme, often referred to as neo-Nazi, right-wing party in West Germany, raised serious doubts as to the way that the *Republikaners* were moving. Many agreed that if the extremists within the party were controlled the Republicans could be a viable political entity.

The year following the comments made by Gerhard Boeden provided additional insight into the interests within the Republican Party. In January 1990, the Federal Office for the Protection of the Constitution classified the *Republikaners* as a party "hostile to the constitution."[23] The reasons given for this indictment were twofold. First, the *Republikaners* were observed using clandestine intelligence-gathering means against their opponents. Second, it was found that 20 percent of the party officials were at one time active in federal or state level right-wing organizations such as the NPD. This accusation, however, did not preclude the Republican Party from participating in West German elections, nor did it keep them from soliciting support in the East German states that were entering into a political union with the Federal Republic.

A cross-section of Republican voters shows that approximately 40 percent voted with the CDU/CSU in 1987. The rest of the voters came from the SPD, with 20 percent, 6 percent from the Greens, 3 percent from the NPD, and 20 percent had not voted in the 1987 elections. This indicates that the Republicans struck a chord with a number of voters across the political spectrum, but that the moderate conservatives took the brunt of the losses.

The true strength of the REP Party has not been fully tested. Only 50 communities out of 1,100 had Republican candidates vying for political posts. In addition, the Republicans have had difficulty developing a meaningful national organization. Those communities that did have REP candidates showed some surprising results. For example, Mannheim, traditionally an SPD stronghold, provided 9 percent of the vote to the Republican candidates. Pforzheim and Heilbronn exceeded 10 percent, Heidenheim over 14 percent, and Freiburg, a university community, over 6 percent. These figures belie a desire by voters to try something different. Long-range viability of these election results may be suspect, but there is a slight move by voters to support portions of the right-wing rhetoric.

The Republican Party faced a factionalism that depleted some of its strength. Internal leadership was severely tested in May 1990. Franz Schönhuber, chairman of the party, resigned after internal conflicts with another powerful *Republikaner*, Harald Neubauer, a former NPD politician. Six weeks later, at the party congress, Schönhuber was reelected as the Republican chairman. This was a result of a vote of confidence by a majority of the remaining representatives after Neubauer and his supporters walked out of the convention. Schönhuber went on to accuse the Bavarian party leadership of Neubauer and his deputy, Franz Glasauer, of pushing the Republican Party into right-wing extremist positions. Schönhuber, who has been consistently attacked for his involvement in the Waffen SS during the war, became sensitive to the REP's political vulnerability if it became apparent that they were obviously supporting right-wing radicalism.

As it is, the Republican Party is treading on the edge of political viability in Germany. Those who tend to show the most support for this rightist party are most sympathetic with the theme of immigrant and asylum-seeker control. Over 85 percent of the REP voters responded to this theme as being the most important. However, opinions concerning the need for limitation of immigration do not differ greatly from those of the CDU.[24] The difference appears to be the methods to be employed and who should be affected.

Ideologically, the Republicans developed a basic program containing three segments. The roughly 13,000 members—as of October 1989—characterize themselves as "an association of German patriots and a liberal and national party with a high social and ecological commitment."[25] This characterization, combined with the three parts of their program, suggests a number of interesting insights into the "real" party.

It is important to note that the Republican Party program is designed for a unified Germany. This is underlined by the importance placed on constitutional order, a viable peace treaty between East and West Germany, reunification, and preservation of the German nation and its ecological living space.

The first section of the program provides an early indicator of the origin and goals of the Republican Party. This is accentuated by the statement that,

the government (present) . . . continues to equate the German past with twelve years of National Socialist rule . . . it is doing nothing to begin the decriminalization of the German culture, history, and people. The war propaganda of the victor powers has gone into our history books and their exaggerations and falsifications must be largely believed by the young people, for an unbiased writing is not yet being made fully possible.[26]

Although claiming patriotism as their primary position, the references to the past and a desire to diminish the importance of events that so encompassed the world and horrified the generations to follow lead some critics to suggest that the Republicans are moving closer to national socialism.

For the most part, the Republican efforts in local elections revolved around law-and-order slogans, fears of economic shortcomings, and alleged foreign threats. Whereas the NPD strengthened during an economic crisis and declined during economic growth, the Republicans strengthened during economic division. This type of economic evolution is predicated on long-term unemployment for a portion of the society and a growing chasm between the wealthy and more well-to-do and the people who are on the edge of subsistence.

The Republican platform provides additional insight into the variations of extremism that were attracted to a new political party. In addition to wanting a reevaluation of German history, the program, as specified in section two, demands a release of all documentation to settle the "sole-blame" thesis, which places responsibility for World War II directly on the National Socialists. This, in itself, appears to suggest that a segment of the party is extremely interested in redefining the historical past of the Nazi influence on Germany and eradicating some of the guilt that has permeated German society since 1945.

Another interesting aspect of the party platform is the language used throughout the document. Many subtle uses of words used during the rise of the NSDAP tend to make one wonder as to the associations of this party to the past Nazi ideology. Such phrases as "Germans of all social strata" and "preserving the continuance of the German people, its health and its ecological *Lebensraum* (living space) as a priority goal of domestic policy," send shivers down the backs of those fearing the growth of the Republican Party's influence. Additionally, terms like *Völk* (German people) and *Völk und Staat* (People and State) are used freely. "Care for and exercise of the ... physical, spiritual, and mental strengths of the youth," bring back memories of the Nazi Youth programs. Although these references may not be designed to infer National Socialist traditions, the perception exists that there are influences within the Republican Party that generate continued right-wing extremism, if not neo-Nazism.

The Republican program can be interpreted in many ways. It is apparent, however, that a sense of the past is still inherent in many who are actively involved in the party hierarchy. Subtle means of communicating this propensity are best evidenced by a television ad run during the 1989 West Berlin House of Delegates election. The ad showed Turkish children playing, while the theme song in the background played "Play the Song of Death." This tasteless approach to campaigning raised a furor, but was indicative of extremist attitudes that permeated the growing Republican Party. Even using this ad, the REP did not fail to gain a small, but viable, political support base in Germany.

Following the show of power in Berlin, the right wing was again capable of expanding their base of influence in local elections in the state of Hesse. The city of Frankfurt, the largest metropolitan area in Hesse, held elections on 12 March 1989. The NPD, for the first time in its history, received 6.6 percent of the local vote, allowing the ultra-Right to occupy seven seats in the Frankfurt parliament.[27] This win constituted a major victory for the political fortunes of a party that had been considered virtually a political nonentity only five years earlier. In 1985, the NPD had only obtained 0.1 percent of the same electorate vote.[28] As was the case in West Berlin, over 4,000 demonstrators protested the NPD's entry into the parliament of Frankfurt.

The basic political platform on which the NPD, CDU-Liste D, CVU, and the Republican Party gained the most popular support was predicated on the question of foreigners. A poll taken in 1981 indicated that 79 percent of the West Germans felt that there were too many foreigners in West Germany.[29] The numbers of foreigners had climbed to over 4.65 million by 1981.[30] This was a 16 percent increase over a three year period and accounted for approximately 7.5 percent of the total West German population by 1980 (see Table 3.1). The Turks dominated the figures of immigration during the last two decades. They accounted for almost 1.5 million of the total immigrants to West Germany and the majority of the Turks tended to enter the bigger German cities, where low-paying jobs were more plentiful (see Table 3.2).

Table 3.1
Foreign Population in West Germany (by nationality)

	1969	1974	1980
Italian	514,600	629,600	617,900
Turkish	332,400	1,027,800	1,462,400
Yugoslavia	331,600	707,800	631,800
Greek	271,300	406,400	297,500
Spanish	206,900	272,700	180,000
Portuguese	37,500	121,500	112,300
Austrian	121,000	177,000	172,600
Dutch	99,100	109,900	107,800

Source: Statisches Bundesamt (Wiesbaden), <u>Statistische Jahrbuch für die Bundesrepublik Deutschland (1969, 1974, 1980)</u>. Note the decreases in all categories of foreigners between 1974 and 1980 except the Turks, who have literally quadrupled in one decade

Many West Germans carried the perception that the foreign-born immigrants were having an adverse impact on German society, which led to a strong negative response from the populace against the government support of immigration. Polls showed a general animosity among the population toward foreigners. A perception existed that these foreigners, particularly the Turks, were welfare cheats who tended to lower educational standards and took jobs needed by Germans in an age of high unemployment.

The facts did not necessarily support these perceptions. For

Table 3.2
Foreign Population in Major West German Cities (1980)

	Total Population	(in thousands) Foreign	Turkish
Munich	1,298,900	218,200 (17%)	39,200 (3%)
Berlin	1,898,900	211,300 (11%)	93,400 (5%)
Hamburg	1,648,800	143,100 (9%)	46,200 (3%)
Cologne	976,800	141,300 (14%)	62,400 (6%)
Frankfurt	629,200	138,800 (22%)	25,500 (4%)
Stuttgart	582,400	105,500 (18%)	18,300 (3%)
Dortmund	609,400	52,800 (9%)	20,600 (3%)

Source: Statische Bundesamt (Wiesbaden), <u>Statische Jahrbuch für die Bundesrepublik Deutschland</u> (1980). Note that Cologne, Berlin, and Frankfurt had the highest percentage of Turks per capita. Two of these cities, Frankfurt and Berlin led the right-wing political resurgence in the early 1989 local elections based on platforms against continued foreign immigration without some method of control.

instance, the numbers of foreign workers dependent on German welfare only amounted to about 8 percent of the active rolls. When comparing the percent of population that the foreigners accounted for (7.5 percent in 1980 and higher in 1989) and the percent of the welfare roles (8 percent) that the foreigners were responsible for, the resultant ratio equals that of the rest of the German employable population. The greater number of foreign workers were, in fact, employed, or were not participants in the German welfare program. However, the foreign worker was most often employed in menial jobs that the average German refused to accept. The unemployment rate for foreigners was 12 percent in 1980 in comparison to 8.2 percent for the Germans, but fewer foreigners were willing to accept social support.[31]

The right-wing proponents levied charges against the Turkish community, including the lowering of educational standards, which provided an emotional issue that gained popular support among many West Germans. One right-wing organization in North Rhine Westphalia went so far as to request a referendum to provide for separate classrooms for foreigners and Germans.[32] Whether the young foreign students have in fact lowered the educational standards across the board has not been definitively proven. The greatest problem has appeared to be in the linguistic skills. The young immigrants are often from families where German is not spoken at home. Therefore, these students have been at a disadvantage in school until they become fluent in their adopted country's language.

The fear of the foreign influence on German education and the perception that jobs were being taken from Germans, provided fertile ground for the ultra-Right, which had for the most part dropped anti-Semitism following World War II. By the 1980s, they had begun to concentrate on the Turks as being the major source of problems in the modern German system. The actual number of Germans who supported this anti-foreign rhetoric was very small in comparison to the total population. However, as Friedrich Hölscher, a member of parliament representing the Free Democrat Party (FDP), said, "the hatred of foreigners is there in a segment of our population."[33] This "hatred" led to an increase in the political fortunes of the NPD, the right-wing coalitions and the newly formed Republican Party, and provided grist for the rising neo-Nazis.

In addition to the larger, more publicized right-wing extremist organizations, there are a number of small fringe groups that contain both militant and ultra-Right elements. The *Gesellschaft für Freie Publizistik* (GFP) encompasses about 100 to 200 members who specifically support a right-wing view involving culture in Germany. This particular group has traditionally supported the NPD candidates throughout West Germany over the past six years. *Die Deutsche Freiheitsbewegung* (DDF) is an extreme militant group that has tended to align themselves with the *Randgruppen*, which is led by Otto-Ernst Remer. Remer is a 75-year-old leader who has specific ties with the Nazi armed forces. He was the commander of the Berlin regiment during the fateful attempt by *Wehrmacht* officers to assassinate Hitler on 20 July 1944. Remer was directly involved in the ultimate suppression of the perceived threat to Hitler following the attempt. Following the war, Otto-Ernst Remer was a principal organizer and twice the leader of the SRP.

Smaller, yet important militant ultra-Right groups include: *Gesellschaft für biologische Anthropologie Eugenik und Verhaltensforschung*, a racist group that fear that foreigners bring health problems such as tuberculosis and cancer when they immigrate to Germany; *Freundiskreis Ulrich von Hutten*, who are strong advocates for the Rudolf Hess legend and claim that "Hess is a monument to the greatness of man"[34]; and the *Hamburger Liste für Ausländerstopp* (HLA), which was organized in 1982 out of those adherents within the NPD who were strongly against foreigners.

Individually, these right-wing extremist groups have not constituted a major political power. However, the recent elections in which these groups, in conjunction with less militant right-wing followings, have coalesced into a small, yet vocal coalition, showed that votes can be obtained throughout West Germany.

THE GROWTH OF MILITANCY

During the early 1970s, the right wing appeared to be incapable of developing a viable political following. The NPD, traditionally the party of the ultra-conservatives, was on the verge of extinction as a political party. Membership dropped to a mere 4,000 by the mid-1970s. West Germany's increased economic strength and standard of living lessened interest in right-wing rhetoric. Those within the party who were interested in the more extreme methods of dealing with Germany's problems became frustrated with the inability of the NPD to gain a viable political position. Many of these members began to drift toward the more extremist organizations that were continually revolving around the fringes of the right-wing political entities. During the 1970s, the extremist groups began to evolve into organizations of some substance, as a greater number of NPD members drifted to the neo-Nazi groups.[35] Out of the estimated 69 identified extremist right-wing political groups in 1988, which had approximately 25,000 members, 220 members were considered actively militant by the government.[36] These militants were identified through records that showed them committing violent crimes, planning acts of violence, or involved in illegal use of weapons, munitions, or bombs.[37]

From the mid-1970s into the 1980s, extremist activities became more visible. The attraction of far-right NPD members to the neo-Nazi groups did not make the neo-Nazis a major movement within Germany, or Europe, but did bring back memories of the Third Reich. This movement that appeared to follow the practices of the Nazi past was not popular among the majority of the German population. The key to the potential of these groups to develop a following revolved around the potential insecurities associated with domestic economics. As unemployment increased, the neo-Nazis attempted to assume the role of "leader" in the fight for better working conditions and job opportunities. They used the traditional Nazi slogans in order to provide the reasons for the German problems associated with recession. Many of the Germans who had been directly effected by the recession became interested in what the extremists were saying. A sense of empathy developed among many West Germans, which laid the foundation for right-wing support in the 1980s. On the other hand, when the economy strengthened, the extremists tended to lose the majority of the audience that was susceptible to right-wing ideology.

Another change that subtly occurred in the 1980s was an opening of German society to the historical perspectives of the Third Reich. This awareness was interpreted by some as a "nostalgic" return to the Nazi past.[38] The Soviet Defense Ministry newspaper, *Krasnaya Zvezda* suggested that German Chancellor Helmut Kohl was partially responsible for the increased interest in the Nazi past. The article argued that the Bonn government allowed the sales of liquor in bottles shaped as a bust of Hitler, closed a school in Bavaria in order for students to attend an exhibition on neo-Nazi activities, and banned the construction of a monument in Hanover that was dedicated to victims of the Nazis.[39]

Of course, these allegations were designed as propaganda and showed the paranoia that existed in the neighboring European countries and the Soviet Union concerning Nazism. Although the situations presented by the Soviets were blown out of proportion, there was still a kernel of truth in the argument. West Germany took a less stringent approach to the anti-Nazi laws during the 1960s and 1970s. The younger Germans needed to realize that the era existed, and that a void in German history left many questions, which led to attempts in many parts of Germany to provide an historical perspective for the Nazi years. Whether this new awareness provided an opening for potential membership in neo-Nazi groups is highly unlikely. The apparent opening of "Pandora's Box" led some critics to blame the new awareness of the "glories" of the Nazi past on local and federal government. These critics suggested that the Federal Republic no longer actively enforced the bans on Nazism that were placed into effect following World War II.

How then, were the neo-Nazi programs able to survive and gain more visibility during the 1980s? Studies within West Germany have indicated that, as of 1980, the influence of ex-

Nazis was still apparent within the more radical fringes of the right wing. Those ex-Nazis that were over 50 years old in the late 1970s and early 1980s became known as visionaries, rather than the center of the "new" awakening of neo-Nazism. These people tended to lean toward a desire to bring back the past and were motivated to retain the old ideas of Nazism. They were, therefore, ill-placed to provide a more contemporary leadership that reflected on the more recent German problems.[40] However, these older radicals had generally maintained strong Nazi convictions and tended to develop vital contacts with German youth that were based on old ideologies.[41]

Many former Nazis gathered frequently and often organized associations that were designed to provide fellowship. These associations were generally developed around past military organizations, the most famous being the Waffen SS. For the most part, the gatherings of the past Nazi officers and soldiers were overlooked by the government, primarily under the assumption that the meetings would be short-lived as the members died. In addition, many within government felt that the tradition of comradeship associated with the military was not necessarily anti-government. Former Waffen SS and Wehrmacht members traditionally met over the decades following the war. These gatherings increased in the 1970s and 1980s, primarily for funerals of passing comrades.[42] Many of these elderly ex-soldiers are still emphatically supportive of the Nazi traditions.

Neo-Nazi organizations of the 1970s and 1980s incorporated the influence of some of these "retired" ex-Nazis. Although normally not directly involved in the extremist activities associated with the neo-Nazis, they were often recognized as supporters of the neo-Nazi ideology, particularly regarding foreigners within Germany.[43]

The more recent neo-Nazi organization memberships are made up primarily of World War II ex-soldiers and young lower middle-class Germans. The elders were often involved in the veteran associations and provided an active reading group for the right-wing neo-Nazi oriented newspaper, *Nationale Zeitung*. This particular newspaper, acting as the primary mouthpiece of the neo-Nazis, is published in Munich and has a circulation of over 100,000.[44] Although not generally active as members of neo-Nazi groups, this war-time generation has provided a constant source of empathy, financial support, and a strong commitment to the ideals of Nazism that has enhanced the efforts of the neo-Nazi leadership to obtain new members.

The younger members are primarily men who are under 30 years of age and tend to be militantly oriented. There have been numerous cases of defamation of property and threats that the hardcore neo-Nazi members perpetrated. Illegal acts were committed that were designed to obtain monies or weapons for bolstering the militancy of the movement. The target audience for membership has been among the working class, rather than the upper middle class student population. Active membership has remained fairly small, but the direct and indirect associations with the elderly Nazi veterans provided a link of continuity that instilled a sense of tradition and a source of ideology for the neo-Nazi movement.

NOTES

1. Kurt Tauber, *Beyond Eagle and Swastika* (Connecticut: Wesleyan University, 1967), 883.

2. Ibid., 884.

3. Walter Laqueur, *The Age of Terrorism* (Boston: Little, Brown, 1987), 83.

4. Tauber, 884.

5. Gordon Craig, *The Germans* (New York: G. P. Putnam's Sons, 1982), 80.

6. Ibid., 80.

7. Ibid.

8. Stephen F. Szabo, "Political Shifts in West Germany," *Current History* (November 1988), 363.

9. Ibid.

10. "International News Section," *Business Week*, 4 April 1988, 53.

11. Ibid.

12. Figures for the district breakdowns of popular votes were obtained from Berger et al., "Movement on the Right Edge: The Small Radical Parties, the Big Winners, Analysis of the Baden-Württemburg Election Results," *Die Zeit* (25 March 1988), 5.

13. Ibid.

14. "Jewish Leader Warns of Neo-Nazi Resurgence in West Germany," *The Reuter Library Report* (22 March 1988).

15. "Unser Endziel in der Bundestag," *Der Spiegel* 6 (6 February 1989), 28.

16. Ibid.

17. Ekkehard Kohrs, "After the Election Results the Great Illusion," *General Anzeiger* (Bonn), 2 February 1989, 3.

18. The Swiss rotation system provides for a foreign worker to work in Switzerland for a specific period of time and then return to his/her native country in exchange for another worker. This program is designed to inhibit permanent residence by the foreign workers, and yet provides a fairly low-cost source of labor.

19. Serge Schmemann, "Far-right Victory Stirs High Anxiety in Berlin," *New York Times*, 31 January 1989.

20. "SPD fordert Verfassungsschutz zur Beobachtung der Republikaner auf," *General Anzeiger*, 3 February 1989, 2.

21. Ibid.

22. "Industrial Body Decries Republikaner Influence," *Frankfurter Rundschau*, 6 October 1989, 24.

23. "Report Finds Republicans Hostile to the Constitution," *The Week in Germany*, 26 January 1990, 2.

24. Ibid.

25. Ibid.

26. Ibid.

27. "CDU Incurs Heavy Losses in Hesse," *The Week In Germany*, 17 March 1989, 1.

28. Ibid.

29. John Vinocur, "Foreign Workers in West Germany Live Under the Shadow of Prejudice," *New York Times*, 22 February 1982, 3.

30. Ibid.

31. Ibid.

32. Ibid.

33. Ibid.

34. Der Minister des Innern, *Verfassungsschutzbericht 1987* (Bonn: Graphische Betriebe GmbH, 1988), 119.

35. Wanda von Baeyer-Katte et al., *Gruppenprozesse* (Opladen: Westdeutscher Verlag GmbH, 1982), 443.

36. Der Minister des Innern, *"Die Herausforderung unseres Demokratischen Rechtsstaates durch Rechtsextremisten,"* 1988, 2.

37. Ibid.

38. "Moscow Says Nostalgia for Nazi Past Sweeping West Germany," *The Reuter Library Report*, 23 January 1987.

39. Ibid.

40. Herbert Jäger et al., *Lebenslaufanalysen* (Opladen: West-deutscher Verlag GmbH, 1981), 111.

41. Ibid.

42. Joan Fischer, "Gatherings of Former Nazis Still Common in West Germany," *Associated Press (International News)*, 21 July 1988.

43. John Ardagh, *Germany and the Germans* (New York: Harper and Row, 1987), 396.

44. Ibid., 395.

4   Profiles of the
        Radical Right

National Socialism will be won back city by city and area by
area.

Michael Kühnen, March 1989

The NPD lost over 20,000 members during the 15 years following the height of its power in 1965. From a low of 4,000
members in the mid-1970s the party leveled out to about 7,000
active members in 1982.[1] Many of the small, and up until 1975,
fairly insignificant neo-Nazi groups benefitted from the decay
of the NPD. Those who left the party and joined the neo-Nazi
organizations brought with them a more militant nature, born
in the frustrations of trying to stay within the "system."

INCREASED EXTREMISM, 1970s and 1980s

The West German right-wing extremists, which included the
more militant neo-Nazis, were drawn almost exclusively from
the lower classes of German society. The dominant membership
was made up of younger, less educated people, who tended to
be laborers. Often these people were not equipped with the
skills necessary to compete in the modern high technology industries that had become prevalent in West Germany during
the 1970s and 1980s. The inability to obtain suitable employ-

ment, and a sense of being displaced by foreigners, pushed many of these young people to radicalism and into the more militant neo-Nazi organizations. They were susceptible to the emotional slogans and facile answers provided by the neo-Nazi leaders, who symbolized authority, support, and stability. Unemployment rates of around 8 percent, with the majority in the lower blue-collar class, provided impetus to the growth of neo-Nazi membership. These young members brought with them a fatalist view of the present economic situation in Germany and a sense of frustration from the inability to obtain meaningful work.

As of May 1988, West German Minister of the Interior Freidrich Zimmerman stated the government's realization that neo-Nazism was increasing and becoming increasingly violent.[2] A 10 percent increase in neo-Nazi membership was estimated to have occurred in just one year from 1987 in 1988.[3] In addition, Zimmerman said that neo-Nazi related acts of violence increased from 71 to 76 over the same period, which was a strong indication of an increasingly discontented right-wing extremism.[4] The young people who were turning to neo-Nazism during this period were venting a frustration against a society that they perceived was unable, or not interested in, solving the problems of the unemployed. This was fueled by the perception that foreigners were receiving more benefits than locals, thereby increasing the tensions among the younger generation.

During the late 1970s the appearance, or increased visibility, of militant extremist organizations became evident. The following groups began to come to the attention of the German legal system: *Aktionsgemeinschaft Nationaler Sozialisten*, led by Michael Kühnen; *Deutsche Aktionsgruppe*, led by Manfred Roeder; *Wehrsportgruppen Hoffman*, led by Karl Heinz Hoffman; and the *Völkssozialistische Bewegung Deutschlands/Partei der Arbeit* (VSBD/PdA), a group of 120 members that called for a youth front and was led by Friedhelm Busse. All of these groups were actively involved in militant neo-Nazi types of incidents. The government attempted to quell the interest in these organizations by incarcerating many of the extremist leaders for varying periods of time, but the organizations did not disintegrate.

The majority of the militant organizations with neo-Nazi leanings evolved ideologically from leaders with long-time activists right-wing backgrounds. Each of the early ideological "gurus" had experienced the Third Reich from the perspective of young men. These ideologists imbued their followers with a philosophy that was predominantly fashioned after the ideology of the NSDAP. Drawing on the symbolism of Nazism, these men developed a following among both young and old.

The key postwar ideologists that insured the continuance of Nazi ideas included men with a wide range of war-time experiences. Supporting the more vocal and extremist ideologists were a number of right-wing intellectuals who provided supportive writings and speeches. The most rabid neo-Nazis included men such as Manfred Roeder, Paul Otte, and Heinrich Eisermann, each of whom perpetuated their ideals within the ultra-rightist environments of the West German political right wing.

Manfred Roeder, leader of the neo-Nazi group *Deutsche Aktionsgruppen*, was born in 1929 and spent the years following the war supporting Nazi traditions and furthering the development of neo-Nazi activities. Paul Otte, the ideologist of a right-wing group called *Braunschweiger Gruppe*, was born in 1924 and was a member of the Wehrmacht from 1942 to 1945. Heinrich Eisermann had been in the German navy and was considered the elder statesman for the neo-Nazi ideology since he had been a Hitler appointee in Schleswig-Holstein. Each of these men provided their own brand of Nazi ideology to the postwar neo-Nazi movement. Each also insured that the postwar youth were exposed to the rigid, but nationalistic ideas that had so deeply penetrated the previous generation. Although the original ideologies provided by these more senior members were steeped in Third Reich tradition, by the 1970s and 1980s the younger members within the neo-Nazi groups, such as Michael Kühnen and Karl Heinz Hoffman, were developing their own followings.

Michael Kühnen, a former lieutenant in the Bundeswehr,

was the driving force in the development of the most visual neo-Nazi organizations in the Federal Republic of Germany during the late 1970s and early 1980s. In the early 1970s he organized the *Nationalistische Front* (NF), the most visible neo-Nazi group in West Germany. Kühnen's overt use of Nazi sloganism and memorabilia placed him at the forefront of the German neo-Nazi movement. He attacked the right of the Allies to remain on German soil, questioned the need for NATO, criticized the government's program for bringing foreign workers into the country, and argued that homosexuality was weakening German society. Kühnen's overt efforts to promote the militant NF resulted in him being sent to prison. By 1985, Meinhoff Schönborn assumed the NF leadership. Kühnen went on to organize another neo-Nazi group called *Aktionsfront Nationaler Sozialisten/Nationale Aktivisten* (ANS/NA), which dominated the militant neo-Nazi movements in the late 1980s.

Kühnen wrote two treatises that he used to identify the goals of his organizations and the ideology upon which his programs were based. These two books, *Die Zweite Revolution* (The Second Revolution) and *Glaube and Kampf* (Faith and War), were not only distributed in Europe, but from 1978 to 1982 were given to neo-Nazi organizations in the United States.[5] In his second book, *Die Zweite Revolution*, Kühnen argued for a need for Aryanism and adamantly supported the NSDAP and the original Nazi paramilitary force, the SA (*Sturmabteilung*).[6] He also supported a Europe under the domination of Germany, which would espouse the fundamentals of anti-Zionism, anti-communism, and anticapitalism.[7] Kühnen became an important leader of neo-Nazism within Germany and gained valuable support from the NPD, in exchange for a political alliance.

Who were susceptible to the die-hard postwar messengers of Nazism? Studies conducted during the immediate postwar period showed that approximately 30 percent of the population in the U.S. occupation zone were considered right extremists, many of whom still considered the NSDAP principle as good.[8] By 1981, a study commissioned by the Bonn government estimated that the numbers of supporters of NSDAP ideology had dropped from the high postwar levels to a mere 13 percent, or approximately 5 million people.[9] The majority of these recently identified right-wing extremist supporters were in the over 50-year-old bracket. These older sympathizers constituted approximately 20 percent of the total 13 percent identified.[10] In addition, semi-skilled workers made up 14.4 percent of the total, the unemployed 13 percent, the self-employed 6.5 percent, and the farmers 14 percent of the 5 million supposed supporters.[11] The balance of those who were identified as having leanings toward the extremists came from a cross-section of German society. What is apparent in considering these statistics is that a core of support for the extremists existed in West Germany from the end of the war until the early 1980s. Although the percentage of supporters declined, the types of people who were associated, or supported the ideology of the extremists, continued to be the small town lower middle class and the rural populations. This is not to say that these people were activists. What is important is that there remained within the population a small number who did not completely deplete either all or portions of Nazi ideology following the war. Time diminished the numbers, but did not erase the dreams and memories of some who had found strength in the programs of the NSDAP.

NEO-NAZI DEMOGRAPHICS

Those who supported the right-wing radical groups, both social and political, tended to fall into similar patterns or profiles. Although a minority of the militants were of different social background, most of those identified by the government fell within general categories.

Sport hooliganism, particularly incidents involving soccer fans, were directly linked to neo-Nazi agitation and recruiting. West German attempts to control outbursts of violence during the international soccer championships in 1988 resulted in charges that right-wing extremists were directly involved in the instigation of such acts. Professor Lode Walgrave, a Belgium academician, compiled a report for the Belgium government that suggested that cross-border links between neo-Nazi groups and so-called hooligans multiplied the danger of joint activities, such as the soccer incidents, and tended to provide new support for the neo-Nazi movements.[12]

The perception, however, that all neo-Nazi members are hooligans and rowdies, with only an interest in vandalism, is misleading. There are deep associations for many who have moved to radicalism. Unemployment, frustrations with life, a sense of devotion to history, a need for authority, and the void left by an economy that moved rapidly into high-tech provided the stimuli for the movement toward militancy.

Right-wing extremist demographics indicate some important information about the present-day right-wing militant. A survey commissioned by the German government in the late 1970s showed the demographic characteristics associated with these right-wing extremists.[13] Most of the respondents, out of a survey audience of approximately 100, said that they had shifted from the NPD to the extremist groups. This was undoubtedly attributable to the near collapse of the NPD in the 1970s and early 1980s. Since the NPD was the only viable political party that supported radical rightist ideologies, this left many frustrated with their remaining options. The majority also said that they unequivocally supported the position of the NSDAP and admired Hitler as the greatest German politician. The consensus from this group was that a democratic parliament was inefficient and ineffectual, therefore, it was better to have a one-party system. The use of power was considered by most of the respondents to be essential at specific times in history when it would best resolve an issue. All of those who responded were outspoken anti-Semitic and anti-Communist. It is interesting to note that all respondents did not respond to every question and tended to be more circumspect about their answers in comparison to left-wing interviewees, who were also surveyed at the same time. What is abundantly clear is that Nazi ideas and history dominated the right-wing extremists in Germany during the early 1980s, which is over 35 years after the supposed demise of Nazism.

The youth who were recruited by these right-wing extremist organizations were generally believed to be psychologically unstable and to have little self-esteem. These generalities were predicated on the facts that many of the youth involved tended to have experienced school failures, job failures, or were chronically unemployed.[14] The psychological patterns that dominated the right-wing extremists suggested that the younger members tended to be alone with their problems and there was no one with whom these young people could release the inherent fears and frustrations that the problems generated. Therefore, these youth found security in the comradeship that came with the militant style of organization associated with the right-wing extremists. The dependency that came with this method of facing problems continued to increase, primarily since there was no positive role model and no social or economic future guaranteed through association with the extremist groups.[15]

The fear among many Germans that the "siren call" of right-wing militarism was making inroads into the postwar generation of German youth led to an interest by professionals dealing with those youth. Theo Pöngsen, a social worker in Bonn, determined a need to provide the young people with alternatives to the right-wing movement. In a lecture, "Right-radicalism by the Youth," Pöngsen argued that a viable nationwide program was necessary that would combat the rising tendency for youth to get involved in right-wing activities.[16] He suggested that as of 1988 there were 14 rightist groups in Bonn alone, which were appealing to an ever-growing number of local youth.[17] Such extremist youth organizations as "Viking Youth" and "Comrades of Bonn/Rhein Sieg" generated support by attending meetings of other youth groups and recruiting actively at those meetings. Soccer clubs also offered excellent opportunities for recruitment as was evidenced by an increase in enrollment of the Dortmund right-wing youth group, "Brussen Front," which actively recruited among the soccer crowds. The overtly active efforts to develop a membership among the youth over the past ten years provided an ever growing foundation for the right-wing and neo-Nazi organizations throughout Germany.

An especially militant and active extremist group that crept into the youth societies of a number of Western nations had members known as "Skinheads." Originally organized in Great Britain, this subculture of extremely radical and violent young

people became quite visible in the 1980s. The "Skinhead" phenomenon was exported from Great Britain to the United States
and Continental Europe. The openness and extremism of these
militants have caused consternation in the regions that have
been subjected to skinhead neo-Nazism.

The skinheads are not considered by most specialists as neo-
Nazis. What is apparent is that these often extremely violent
youth are incorporated into neo-Nazi groups as "soldiers."
Many are intrigued by the neo-Nazi militarism and the symbolism associated with the Nazi past. This leads to opportunities for violence, justified by the need to "protect" meetings
or to strike against minorities who are deemed available targets for the soldiers, because of the right-wing ideology dealings
with foreigners, anti-Semitism, and anticommunism.

The skinhead's blatant disregard for law and order engen-
dered a fear of a reawakening of the violent excesses that many
still associate with Hitler's regime. Within West Germany the
skinhead subculture has been primarily associated with the
Nationalistischen Front (NF), led by Meinhoff Schönborn, and
the *Freiheitlichen Deutschen Arbeitepartei* (FAP), a fairly recently organized group that incorporated members of the recently banned National Gathering (NS) group. Heinz Reiss, a
leading member of the NS, was elected chairman of the new
FAP, thereby providing continuity to the militant movement.

Within the overall umbrella of the right-wing NF and FAP,
small groups of radicals thrived on neo-Nazi ideology. One of
these groups, called *Jugendliche Randgruppen*, is led by Andreas Pohl, a 27-year-old who is extremely militant. This group
is considered to be the primary skinhead organization in West
Germany associated directly with neo-Nazis. In 1987, the Bonn
government estimated that this group alone had between 200
and 250 active militant members within Germany.[18] Total
membership in this extremist organization was estimated to
be as high as 2,500.[19] These types of militant groups provided
the basis for increased extremism and militancy within the
neo-Nazi organizational structures. The members of such active organizations became associated with right-wing terror
and harassment in the early 1980s. Many of these same people
are now carrying the banner of Germany for an international

neo-Nazi movement that exists in the United States, Western Europe, and South America.

RIGHT-WING VERSUS LEFT-WING MILITANTS

The neo-Nazis tried to incorporate images of the past Nazi triumphs in order to give themselves a sense of credence in modern postwar Germany. The leadership provided a sense of tradition and an ideology that was designed to attract those who wanted to see Germany returned to its once prominent position of power in central Europe. Nationalism was stressed and the importance of returning Germany to the Germans was used as a catalyst to gain support, especially among the youth. By glorifying the symbols of Hilter's Third Reich, the neo-Nazis attempted to fill a void in German history and, at the same time, give the economically disadvantaged an opportunity to express their dissatisfaction within a closed group of commonality. In essence, the neo-Nazis were reinstituting the "old ideas" of the NSDAP, which were glorified as being the foundation for the best years for Germany in the twentieth century.[20]

Demographically, the right-wing extremists provided an interesting comparison to their rivals in the left wing. The right-wing extremist leaders of the 1980s fell into two major age categories. Forty-four percent of the new neo-Nazi leaders were born between 1951 and 1955.[21] The youth that has become dominant in this movement is exemplified by the fact that 56 percent of the 1980s leadership was born after 1956.[22]

The evolving right-wing extremists leadership brought into the movement a potent youthful energy, one that had no direct memory of the excesses of Hitler's Nazism. On the other hand, the left wing has been dominated by leaders who have developed support and contacts over a period of time, making the organizations more distinctly traditional and often very effective.

Membership in the recent neo-Nazi groups was found to be centered on a desire by the young to "belong." Over 44 percent of the youth involved in the right-wing extremist groups, who

agreed to respond to a government commissioned survey, said
that belonging to a group in which comradeship was stressed
was their main reason for becoming members.[23] Another 44
percent claimed that the ideology and the emotional attachment were the key elements for their involvement.[24] The sense
of belonging, and the need to unequivocally accept the neo-
Nazi ideology, provided the foundation for the majority of members in the movement. These were strong factors that often
provided the leadership of these groups with a viable and emotional membership that could be manipulated with careful
propaganda and maintenance of a close knit, self-sufficient
organization.

Recent studies of the membership of the right-wing extremist
youth groups show that the majority of the radicals tended to
place their material existence above the more theoretical needs
of a movement.[25] The study showed that in comparison to only
one left-wing respondent, 62 right-wing respondents claimed
that individual materialistic needs were the most important
requirement. This majority of right-wing responses also correlated with the large number that said that their parents were
also interested primarily in material existence.[26] This relationship becomes clearer when one recognizes that the majority
of the rightists came from small bourgeoisie families that traditionally have had a definitive interest in material needs and
in their professional positions within society. This is further
exemplified in the statistic that showed that 42 percent of the
right-wing respondents came from families in which the bread-
winner was a self-employed craftsman or a small business-
man.[27] In comparison, only five left-wing respondents were
from these types of home environments.

The tendency of the lower-middle class to be the primary
recruit for the right-wing extremists was epitomized in the
statistics that compare education of the rightist and leftist
extremist. In 1980, out of a survey of approximately 75 right-
wing extremists and 75 left-wing extremists, it was found that
only ten right-wingers had middle class educations, in comparison to 69 from the left wing.[28] The working class was represented by nine right-wing adherents, but absolutely no left-
wing respondents.[29] Ten of the rightists were children of par-

ents who were employed by small to medium businesses, whereas, once again, no left-wing respondents were represented.[30] Four of the right wing were from families in which the father was employed in the civil service, in comparison to none for the left.[31] Apparent in these statistics is that the dominant number of right-wing extremists traditionally came from lower middle class environments. The predominant number of left-wing extremists have tended to come from the upper middle class and are often afforded the opportunity to pursue middle class educational goals, which often lead them to the universities.

Unlike the leftist extremists, the neo-Nazi organizations are male oriented. The few women whom the government identified as supporters of the neo-Nazis generally fulfilled the traditional roles of bride, wife, or mother.[32] The women's involvement in the activities of the neo-Nazis usually was indirect, rather than direct. Their identifiable participation normally consisted of moral support for the men and maintenance of the traditional values that were promulgated during the NSDAP's years in power. These values included the responsibility of the home, appropriate raising of the children, and secondary participation in a society dominated by men.

H. D. Schwind, in his book *Ursachen des Terrorismus der Bundesrepublik* (Causes for Terrorism in the Federal Republic), profiled the right-wing radical of the 1980s. These profiles utilized psychological surveys in order to develop trends among the active membership in the more militant organizations. Approximately 97.6 percent of the respondents indicated an extremely close attachment to their mothers, fathers, or another immediate family member.[33] The majority showed a clear interest in maintaining close familial relationships that provided a strong source of mutual support. Another interesting factor that was discovered in Schwind's study was the relationship of the right-wing radicals with the family structure. Approximately 11.9 percent of the respondents indicated that they did not hate their mothers, yet 30 percent claimed to hate their fathers.[34] In comparison, 85.7 percent of the left-wing respondents hated their mothers and only 13 percent hated their fathers.[35] The respondents from the right-wing radicals and from the left-wing were almost diametrically opposed in the family relationship. The rightists showed far more of a tendency for a need for a close family relationship and were far more maternally oriented, whereas the leftists appeared to be more paternally oriented and tended to be less interested in embracing a close family environment.

In addition to familial evaluations, Schwind went on to provide insight into ideological issues that were generally followed by the majorities of both extremist movements. He found during interviews that often the right-wing extremists still actively supported racist policies that were the hallmark of Nazism since the 1920s. Over 50 percent of the right-wing respondents in Schwind's study felt that the "Bolsheviks" (their term for modern Communists) and world Jewry were the major impediments in the economic development of Germany.[36]

Support of Schwind's study was provided through a study commissioned by the Anti-Defamation League of B'nai B'rith, an international Jewish organization headquartered in New York. Over 2,102 interviews were conducted within the German population in regards to personal feelings about Jews.[37] The interviews were conducted by the Institute for Demography in Allensbach, Baden-Württemburg, West Germany during 1987 and early 1988. What was found was a distinct anti-Jewish sympathy within the survey population that was over 60 years of age, which had limited education, lower level occupations, and were from rural or small village environments. Approximately 12 percent of the respondents that fit into this category tended to harbor the anti-Jewish feelings and, in addition, had a distinct distrust of other minorities.[38] In contrast to the elders, only 3 percent of those under 30 years of age supported these same biases.[39] In a similar survey conducted in 1949, 10 percent of the survey population were demonstratively anti-Jewish, 13 percent had negative views, and another 15 percent were reserved in wanting to deal with the Jewish minority.[40] The most recent surveys showed that a greater portion of the generation that had directly experienced the Third Reich continued to maintain a semblance of prejudice against Jews and foreigners. The younger people have not developed the anti-Jewish biases displayed by the earlier generations, but a small number still carry the prejudices of the past. The neo-Nazis have capitalized on this small number of younger people and have used the basis of foreign immigration and workers as the springboard to foment a new distrust, particularly against the Turkish community.

Within West Germany it was found through government studies that right-wing extremism was not wholly a movement of the unemployed or less privileged. Of the identified neo-Nazis—not necessarily those identified as active militants— there were a number of individuals who were officials in the different *Länder*, or states, and minor members within the federal civil service. Out of 86 state officials identified as being neo-Nazi during 1987, 33 were school teachers, eight were judicial justices, seven were in financial divisions, and nine were police.[41] Within the official federal offices, a total of 234 individuals were identified as being neo-Nazi supporters. These included 129 civil servants, 26 soldiers, 46 clerks, and 33 workers.[42] These particular numbers reflect an increase of ten people over the 1986 report who were employees of the federal government and yet maintained active involvement in neo-Nazi groups within West Germany. The numbers of neo-Nazi organizations dropped from 23 in 1986 to 20 in 1987. Although there was a drop in numbers of groups, the numbers of participants increased by 14 percent.

The total number of right-wing extremist groups, as identified by the government officials, dropped from 73 to 69 during the same period. This figure includes the neo-Nazis as well as other organizations that revolve around the fringes of moderate and radical-wing parties. As was the case with the neo-Nazis, the drop in the numbers of so-called right-wing extremist groups did not reflect an overall decrease in membership. An increase was shown in the aggregate membership of right-wing extremist groups between 1986 and 1987. Government estimates placed the total probable number of active right-wing radicals during 1986 as 22,100.[43] By comparison, in 1987, that number was increased to 25,200.[44] This, of course, was only a small minority (0.4 percent) when one considers the total estimated West German population in 1987 at 61.5 million.

In comparing the types of people that are associated with the

Table 4.1
Educational Levels (highest level attained)

SCHOOL LEVEL	Right-wing	Left-wing
Volkschule (Elementary)	49%	17%
Mittel, Fach & Handelsschule		
(Middle, Trade & Business)	22%	15%
Gymnasium (Advanced High School)	17%	19%
Hochschule (Pre-College)	10%	42%
University	2%	7%

Source: Baeyer-Katte et al, Gruppenprozesse (Bonn, 1982), 450.
Note: The numbers of answers to the queries varied between the right and left. Of the right-wing respondents only fifty-one answered this question compared to two hundred twenty-seven left-wing respondents. It would be probable that additional right-wing responses would tend to support the present ratio.

neo-Nazis, there are some educational generalities that can also be drawn. Government officials and specialists felt that a large number of the active participants in the neo-Nazi groups were less educated, lower class individuals with a desire to belong to an organization offering a semblance of stability and authority. The few intellectuals who were identified as active neo-Nazis tended to come from the physical sciences, such as engineering, physics, chemistry, and medicine, along with an extremely limited number of lawyers.[45]

This profile is quite different from that which is normally associated with the left-wing extremists. Studies of the participants in such groups as the Baader-Meinhof, the Red Army Faction, and the Red Cells, have concluded that these people tend to be more educated, often with university level training, and were primarily involved in the social sciences. Table 4.1 provides a sample of the survey results that researchers for the West German government obtained in the early 1980s. This table compared the educational levels of right-wing extremists who were questioned and their left-wing counterparts. The information did not break out the neo-Nazis from the other identified right-wing extremists, however the information provides some insight into the general right-wing extremist profile. Out of a total of 51 right-wing respondents, in comparison to 227 left-wing respondents, the higher level of schooling reflected a lesser number of participants that achieved that level.

In 1981 another demographic study was done with only supposed right-wing terrorists (neo-Nazis). This study found that out of 23 extremists questioned, 11 graduated from *volkschule*, five attended *handelsschule* (only two graduated), three attended *gymnasium* (none graduated), and two went to *hochschule*, but did not graduate.[46] This ratio supported the cross-section of right-wing extremists that were interviewed the following year. These figures lend credence to the argument that the average participant in the right-wing extremist groups, which includes the neo-Nazis, tend to be of lower educational backgrounds.

As was mentioned earlier, the majority of militant activists from the right wing were identified as members of neo-Nazi organizations. These groups were predominantly made up of males. As of 1981, there were no women included in the category of militant extremists within the neo-Nazis, nor other right-wing extremist groups, according to the government studies. On the other hand, 33 percent of the left-wing activists, referred to as terrorists by the government, were women.[47]

The right-wing extremists fall into age categories where a majority of the members were born prior to 1945 (35 percent) and after 1956 (44 percent).[48] By comparison, the left-wing extremists interviewed were primarily born in equal increments from prior to 1945 (34 percent), 1946 to 1950 (34 percent), and 1951 to 1955 (29 percent).[49] Only 3 percent of the leftists were identified as being born after 1956. These numbers show that the right-wing extremists were either older, between 43 years of age and older, or younger, at least 33 and younger. This provided an adequate number of young recruits that were the future leaders and primary activists within the right-wing extremists, including the neo-Nazis, and insured the continuation of rightist ideology.

Another study provided more definition to this age differential. Baeyer-Katte and associates found that in 1981 approximately 51 percent of the right-wing extremists queried were born in 1965 or later.[50] This suggested that the population of the right-wing extremists, including neo-Nazis, were much younger than was initially estimated, prior to the more specific studies. A closer look at the elderly members showed that ap-

Table 4.2
Age Distribution

Birthyear	Right-wing	Left-wing
1965-later	51%	3%
1951-1965	12%	29%
1946-1950	4%	34%
1945-earlier	33%	34%
Before 1930	12%	0%
Number of respondents	51	223

Source: Baeyer-Katte et al, Gruppenprozesse (Opladen, 1982), 448.
Note: Those right-wing extremists that were included in the interview were predominantly considered neo-Nazi by the officials and considered themselves as members of specific neo-Nazi groups.

proximately 12 percent were born before 1930 (see Table 4.2). This exemplified the relationship that existed between the older Nazi generation and the newer neo-Nazi generation.

There was no evidence found that the concepts of Nazism were handed down from generation to generation.[51] In fact, in many cases the youth—generally grandsons—rejected their grandparent's or parent's involvement in the Nazi Party and the associated events. This rejection often manifested itself in a strongly anti-Nazi attitude. Most evidence suggests that the ex-Nazis who continued to hang onto the fringes of the right wing over the four decades following the war provided a base for neo-Nazi evolution in the 1970s and 1980s. These principals insured that the Nazi ideology was carried within the confines of the political parties and was communicated to those who were more susceptible in later generations. Men like Manfred Roeder and Michael Kühnen used these concepts to develop their own brand of neo-Nazism among a growing group of disenchanted youth that was looking for a sense of authority and a reason for venting their frustrations against the central government.

The steady rise in numbers of neo-Nazis over the decade of the 1970s, as evidenced by Table 4.3, and the continued interest in publications provided by these groups suggest that neo-Nazism and other right-wing extremists provided a viable threat to German democracy throughout the latter part of the 1980s.

Table 4.3
Numbers of Right-Wing and Neo-Nazi Members and
Publications

	1976	1977	1978	1979	1980	1984
Right-wing						
Groups	85	83	76	69	75	n/a
Members	18,300	17,800	17,600	17,300	19,800	22,100
Neo-Nazis						
Activists	600	900	1000	1400	1800	1310
Hard-liners	150+	150+	200	300	300	230
Groups	15	17	24	23	22	34
Publications						
R/W Total						
Number	109	99	104	92	85	42*
Circulation	178,300	189,000	178,100	174,300	159,700	

*Only refers to neo-Nazi publications, (i.e. books, newspapers and journals). Note: An
increase of fourteen percent in readership occurred between 1986 and 1987 according to the
Minister of Interior, in his yearly report, _Verfassungsschutzbericht, 1987_, page 98.

Source: Baeyer-Katte et al, Gruppenprozesse, 443.

The lower figures in the mid-1980s showed a decline from the
high numbers of activists in 1980, but remained fairly stable
with only modest increases throughout the remainder of the
decade. Recent reports by the minister of interior showed increased figures in 1987 for most of the categories. For example,
there were 69 right-wing extremist organizations identified by
the government in 1987. This was six less than in 1980, but
the 1980 figures included a few that were banned during the
early part of the decade, and did not reflect the increase in
actual membership. Most of this increase was in the period
from the end of 1986 through 1987. Neo-Nazi numbers grew
as well. In 1987, the total number of identifiable neo-Nazis was
estimated to be about 2,100. Of this 2,100, an estimated 1,380
were considered to be active in neo-Nazi groups.[52] The numbers
of hard-liners, or what could be considered the most militant
(sometimes referred to as the terrorist element) has not
changed much over the past decade. The government still estimates that there are about 200 of these hard-line extremists
active in neo-Nazi programs.[53]

NOTES

1. Hans Josef Horchem, "European Terrorism: A German Perspective," *Terrorism* 6, 1 (1982), 29. Another source by David Carlton and Carlo Schaerf, eds., *Contemporary Terror* (London: Macmillan, 1981), 165, estimated only 4,000 members by 1981. Although the editors argue that a smaller number of actives were involved, they do support the general thesis that many of the members had come from the NPD and had increased the militancy of the neo-Nazi groups that they joined.

2. *Reuters News Summary*, 26 May 1988.

3. Ibid.

4. Ibid.

5. Der Bundesminister des Innern, *Verfassungsschutzbericht, 1987* (Bonn: Graphische Betriebe GmbH, 1988), 100.

6. Ibid.

7. Ibid.

8. Eva Kolinsky, "Terrorism in West Germany," in *The Threat of Terrorism*, ed. Juliet Lodge (Colorado: Westview Press, 1988), 71.

9. Ibid.

10. Ibid.

11. Ibid.

12. John Kampfner, "Orderly West Germany Braced for Invasion of (Soccer) Fans," *The Reuter Library Report*, 19 April 1988.

13. H. D. Schwind, *Ursachen des Terrorismus der Bundesrepublik* (Berlin: Walter de Gruyter, 1978), 102.

14. *"Neofaschismus nicht Verharmlosen," General Anzeiger (Bonn)*, 21 December 1988, 7.

15. Ibid.

16. Ibid.

17. Ibid.

18. Der Bundesminister des Innern, *Verfassungsschutzbericht, 1987*, 120.

19. Bundesminister des Innern, *"Die Herausforderung unseres Demokratischen Rechtsstaates durch Rechtsextremisten,"* 1988, 8.

20. Wanda von Baeyer-Katte et al., *Gruppenprozesse* (Opladen: Westdeutscher Verlag GmbH, 1982), 448.

21. Herbert Jäger, Gerhard Schmidtchen, Lieselotte Süllwold, *Lebenslaufanalysen* (Opladen: Westdeutscher Verlag GmbH, 1981), 70.

22. Ibid.

23. Ibid.

24. Ibid.

25. Schwind, 108.
26. Ibid.
27. Ibid.
28. Ibid., 109.
29. Ibid.
30. Ibid.
31. Ibid.
32. Kolinsky, 77.
33. Schwind, 104.
34. Ibid.
35. Ibid.
36. Ibid., 109.
37. "Anti-Semitism Today," *The Week in Germany*, 8 June 1988, 7.
38. Ibid.
39. Ibid.
40. Ibid.
41. Ibid., 99.
42. Ibid.
43. Ibid., 98.
44. Ibid.
45. Kolinsky, 77.
46. Jäger et al., 111.
47. Ibid., 23.
48. Ibid.
49. Ibid.
50. Baeyer-Katte et al., 448.
51. The author was unable to find a definitive study of genealogical relationships by which the Nazi ideology was specifically passed to children and grandchildren. The potential for a study of this kind is good and would be an interesting facet to the question of how Nazism continues to surface in German society. From the available material, and lacking a social familial study, it appears that contacts between World War II military veterans, normally associated with SS units, and the younger right-wing German radicals were the primary means of continuing the Nazi ideology. This was often accomplished through fringe political party associations.
52. Der Bundesminister des Innern, *Verfassungsschutzbericht, 1987*, 100.
53. Ibid.

5   The Radical Right and Terrorism

One of the most interesting yet least known developments in Western Europe during the last twenty-four months (1977–1979) has been the steady increase in terrorist operations by neo-Nazi groups in the Federal Republic of Germany.

Risks International, Inc.,
Executive Risk Assessment 1, no. 7 (May 1979), 3.

The right-wing extremists, and in particular the neo-Nazis, brought back painful memories to many who endured Hitler's Third Reich. The rise in militant right-wing extremism during the 1980s showed that terrorist activities were not confined to the radical left. Bank robberies, weapons seizures, bombings, and physical violence became the means by which the ultra-rightist expressed their political ideologies. Although not as sophisticated in method, nor as frequent as the leftist activities, the right-wing actions brought the realization to the West German authorities that the Right was susceptible to terrorist involvement.

The West German government traditionally viewed right-wing extremists in West Germany as criminals, rather than as terrorists. This difference was reflected in the manner used to handle judiciary procedures dealing with right-wing transgressions of federal laws. Until the mid-1980s, those right-wing extremists that the government classified as neo-Nazis, and who were arrested for illegal activities, were generally treated as common criminals. This approach was important in that it tended to downplay the connections of the accused with a particular neo-Nazi group, thereby decreasing the potential for the media to develop a group identity.

With the increasingly overt activities that were attributed to the neo-Nazis during the 1980s, the West German government realized that the extreme right wing posed a potential terrorist threat (as opposed to criminal) within West Germany. Because of this change in attitude, officials showed increased interest in dealing with neo-Nazi militants. Beginning in the fall of 1988, the West German government approached the problem of both left-wing and right-wing terrorism in much the same way. The authorities no longer referred to the illegal acts perpetrated by these extremists as acts of terrorism, but they considered terrorist incidents by both sides as purely criminal acts. This was designed to eliminate the media hype that seemed to be associated with the fad word "terrorism."

Can the right-wing extremists be classified as terrorists? Terrorism itself is a vague concept that has become a popular term among social scientists and criminologists over the past 15 years. There are well over 200 different definitions of terrorism, which makes the term somewhat difficult to associate with any particular act or acts. However, in considering the generally accepted key elements that would identify an act as terrorist, many of the actions that were committed by the rightist militants, particularly the neo-Nazis, could be classified as acts of terrorism.

The *Oxford Universal Dictionary* defines terrorism as the "state of being terrified or greatly frightened; intense fear, fright or dread." This particular definition is so general that the modern view of terrorism has transcended the generalists' approach and required more specific verbiage. Bernard Saper, in his article "On Learning Terrorism," attempted to provide a more specific definition of what terrorism in modern society entails. He defined terrorism as "an act or program of life-threatening intimidation, horrible violence, savage armed struggle, holy war, or no-holds-barred battle for national lib-

eration, deliberately, albeit randomly, directed against inno-
cent civilians."[1]

This definition excludes the more definitive considerations
associated with state terrorism, which more recently have become important areas of study. Saper provided a definition of
terrorism that implies that only outwardly savage acts are to
be considered as terrorist in nature. However, intimidation of
populations through selective acts of violence and intimidation
using lesser violence became trademarks of many "terrorist"
groups over the past 50 years. Christopher Dobson and Ronald
Payne, in their studies of terrorist organizations, methods, and
equipment defined terrorism as "the use of violence for political
ends, and includes any use of violence for the purpose of putting
the public or any section of the community in fear."[2] The U.S.
Army defined terrorism as "the calculated use of violence or
the threat of violence to attain political goals through instilling
fear, intimidation or coercion and usually involves a criminal
act often symbolic in nature and intended to influence an audience beyond the immediate victims."[3] These definitions have
some common elements that continually appear. Many of those
who study modern terrorism tend to agree that terrorist activities invariably use violence to obtain recognition. This violence is not predictable, therefore making the potential act
difficult to thwart. Terrorists most often use the violent act to
gain media notoriety, therefore hopefully forcing the population to succumb to fear. Most writers dealing with modern
terrorism accept the thesis that terrorist acts in today's society
revolve around political goals.

Terrorism, therefore, as a term of substance is a rather neb-
ulous method of defining politically motivated violent acts that
are designed to obtain media coverage, or spread fear locally.
Violence is used to cause the general population to yield to the
terrorist's demands or to sympathize with the terrorist's cause.

Reviewing the activities of the neo-Nazis within Germany
and, peripherally, in the Tyrolian region of Italy, many of the
elements associated within the definition of terrorism were
used to attract public awareness. This was epitomized in the
use of bombings, physical assault, and desecration of tradi-

tional religious and governmental monuments in order to force the general population to bow to the interests of the minority Nazi opinions. Over the past decade, and particularly the period from 1985 to 1989, the neo-Nazis enjoyed vastly increased media coverage throughout West Germany, as local newspapers in a number of cities and national magazines picked up the stories of activities. This awakening of the journalists to the phenomenon of modern Nazism caused a certain amount of consternation within the government and in the population. The openness that many of the neo-Nazi groups displayed in the mid-1980s reminded numerous older Germans of a past that many felt was best forgotten.

Joining with the less militant, yet still ultra-right political parties, such as the NPD and Republicans, the neo-Nazis were able to develop a limited political base during the early 1989 elections. Incidents of violence were reduced during this period, as the extremists attempted to incorporate their ideas through the political system. This change to more democratic methods did not eliminate the bank robberies, illegal international sales of equipment and arms, and the use of Gestapo methods for intimidating the populace. These techniques, although appearing to have been set aside in 1989 for the local elections, still remained viable options. This was evidenced by the police raids in early 1989 that produced weapons and Nazi propaganda from many of the followers of Michael Kühnen's neo-Nazi organization.

The Western democracies' tendencies to place more emphasis on the left-wing terrorist menace provides an interesting question. The answer to this question may lie in the initial introduction of the Western nations to terrorism in Europe. During the 1960s, the Baader-Meinhof gang provided a new perspective on terrorism. This small group of disenchanted young people set the stage for the future terrorism that plagued West Germany throughout the 1970s and 1980s. A continuous cycle of terrorist activity from the Left was perpetrated during this period, even with the capture, and ultimately the suicides of the key personages in this group. Today, this activity is primarily embodied in the "Red Army Faction," a mutation of the original Baader-Meinhof organization. As the 1980s dawned, the more militant right-wing groups began using terrorist activities most often associated with the leftist groups. The West German government normally classified these acts as individual crimes, although the use of terrorism by the neo-Nazis tended to be more indiscriminate and caused far greater numbers of death and injury than those conducted by the left-wing groups. Specific violent incidents were, in fact, considered acts of terrorism. These were the exception rather than the rule when dealing with right-wing actions. An example was the bombing at *Octoberfest* in 1980, which injured over 200 people and killed 13. Again, in 1984, an attack on a Munich disco was classified as a terrorist action. Other than these two major violent acts, right-wing violence was considered purely criminal, unless arson or burglary were used to obtain monies or munitions.

What other factors may have influenced the Western nations to focus on the Left and, for the most part, ignore the right-wing militants? The 1960s and early 1970s were periods of youth unrest. The "New Left" subculture of the 1960s influenced youth in the United States and in Western Europe. In Germany, a growing disenchantment among some of the youth began to develop during the mid-1960s. The negative opinions of these young people evolved because of the awareness of the potential dangers of nuclear weaponry and the continuous presence of foreign troops on West German soil. The left wing began to attract some of the middle and upper class youth, who saw these political options as not acceptable for the future of Germany. The radicalization of many of these young people was caused by the apparent inability of the political organization to quickly change "the system." Germany began to receive attention as a bed of terrorism as the Baader-Meinhof gang used terrorism on a regular basis. Even after the elimination of Andreas Baader and Ulriche Meinhof, along with other leaders within their group, a second and third generation of left-wing terrorists took their place. The amount of press coverage and the boldness of the attacks placed these groups in the forefront of terrorism in Europe. This led to antiterrorist efforts on the part of the German government that are today some of the most effective in the world. New laws were passed by the Parliament that directly affected terrorist activity in Germany, making it more difficult to obtain hiding places and to obtain passive support. These new laws also provided for more stringent police and judicial procedures, which tended to infringe on individual rights. The Federal Republic of Germany placed the effort on fighting terrorism perpetrated by the left-wing extremists and developed judicial procedures and methods of combatting subversion that were directly related to these types of groups.

Arms and money were readily available during the 1970s and 1980s for many of the extremist organizations. This became obvious as many of the members of militant groups from both the Right and Left were arrested and interrogated. Both sides used international connections to obtain weapons and funds, which generally increased the effectiveness and the support base of their terrorist activities. Yonah Alexander, a noted specialist in terrorism, suggested that the international controls that were in effect in the mid-1980s were "far too weak, which often gave the terrorists a sense of security."[4] Definitions of terrorism and methods of combatting terrorist acts varied from country to country, making it extremely difficult to develop concerted multi-national efforts to control terrorism.

As stated earlier, during the late 1960s and early 1970s, the neo-Nazis were such a small minority that their activities were almost mute. The old advocates of the Nazi era dominated these neo-Nazi organizations and fashioned them after the NSDAP. By the late 1970s and early 1980s, these organizations began to evolve under a new generation of leaders who saw a need for changes within the groups and within German society. These newer leaders did not see capitalism as the primary focus for their attacks, but saw the Bonn government as an ineffectual behemoth that was unable to throw off the "mantel" of occupation and was susceptible to the increasing trend of foreign immigration. The neo-Nazis placed emphasis on the need to eject the "occupation forces" and return Germany to her rightful place as a principal sovereign power in Europe. In order to fight the apparent weakness of the Federal Republic's government, the neo-Nazis began to mobilize popular support against the continuation of liberal government policies concerning foreign workers. In addition, German nationalism was stressed and active efforts were directed against U.S. soldiers, foreign businesses, and foreign military installations.[5] The United States Defense Intelligence Agency regarded the right-wing militants in Germany as extremists who specifically opposed the existing government in Bonn and were against the U.S. military presence in Germany.[6]

The West German government categorized a number of neo-Nazi groups as criminally militant, after a number of terrorist activities were tied to these organizations in the early 1980s. Reports of attacks against U.S. military personnel and North Atlantic Treaty Organization (NATO) facilities and personnel surfaced during this period and were linked to right-wing extremists.[7] A strong opposition to the U.S. presence in West Germany, which the right-wing referred to as "occupation," and a general disgust with the Western alliance (NATO), led to an increasing number of incidents during the early 1980s. Once the apparent sanctuary of the "left-wing" terrorists, the right wing showed a flair for militancy as well. Of interest is the fact that the neo-Nazis professed to be strongly anti-Communist, yet they never attacked Communist, Socialist or Soviet targets. The neo-Nazi efforts appeared to be purely directed against the foreign forces that were stationed in West Germany. By using activism and violence, the "new" neo-Nazi attempted to shock the population back to the age of the Third Reich and in doing so generate a popular surge for change among the German public. The decade of the 1980s was the period of increased right-wing militancy. West Germany became acutely aware of the growth of a new breed of neo-Nazi, many of whom were not afraid of openly expressing their views and using terrorist methods to obtain publicity.

Neo-Nazi terrorist activity increasing during the early 1980s should not have surprised the democratic nations. As was shown, Allied efforts at eliminating the Nazi ideology after the war were not particularly successful. A rising number of right-wing radicals, by the mid-1970s, began to arrive at the same conclusions as those of the youth of the 1960s. Political impotence plagued the strongholds of right-wing sympathies such as the NPD Party and far-right fringes of the CDU and CSU.

This led to a radicalization on the right that became evident in the 1980s. In the early part of the decade, these groups of disenchanted people found that their efforts to restore the German past via political means were ineffectual. Therefore, new methods were tried that were hauntingly familiar. Similar to the violent efforts utilized by the Nazis, the neo-Nazis used techniques of harassment and threats. Bold acts of terrorism and outright flaunting of the postwar laws, which were passed to protect the country from a return of Nazism, became far more prevalent. The neo-Nazis used methods that were fairly unsophisticated and, therefore, did not receive the notoriety accorded the left wing. These early efforts forced the neo-Nazi groups, particularly those under the leadership of Michael Kühnen, to reconsider the benefits derived from terrorism and pushed them toward utilization of the existing political system. These neo-Nazis, by joining with the extremist right-wing parties (NPD and REP), were able to provide initial support for right-wing candidates.

What was the major impediment to the neo-Nazis gaining the notoriety and attention as terrorists that was given to the leftist organizations? The major reasons that the West German government identified the neo-Nazi extremists as common criminals, rather than terrorists, appeared to be a combination of factors. First, the militant neo-Nazi extremists did not begin overt violent activities that were of interest to the media until the late 1970s and early 1980s. Prior to this time, the extremist activities that were normally associated with the neo-Nazi cliques were largely limited to clandestine meetings, numerous incidents of anti-Semitic and anti-foreign harassment, and a sense of nostalgia for the "Third Reich." The German government banned these neo-Nazi organizations when they stepped beyond the limits of minor infractions of the laws that prohibited pro-Nazi activities. The West German government's realization in the early 1980s that the right-wing had a fairly large following, and that the neo-Nazis were becoming more open about their activities, led to a reevaluation of the actual threat that the far right posed in the German democracy.

A less direct, yet significant, difference that tended to keep the right-wing neo-Nazi militants from being classified as terrorists and receiving stiffer penalties was the neo-Nazis's attitude that was demonstrated in their court appearances. Whereas the leftist terrorist often rebelled in the courtroom and tended to cause continuous discomfiture to the officials, those neo-Nazis charged with crimes normally projected a sense of order and a proper acceptance of authority. The accused often dressed conservatively and appropriately, maintained a clean-cut appearance, and generally showed respect to the judicial officials. This appearance of socially acceptable behavior frequently weighed in favor of the accused and often resulted in lesser punishments. By approaching authority in a manner that was acceptable, the neo-Nazi was considered by authorities to be a member of society, although they may have committed an illegal act. What is implicated in the mannerisms shown by these neo-Nazis who were accused of crimes was a philosophy that was inherent in the far-right ideology. The neo-Nazis were immersed in the importance of authority, simply because of their support of authoritative rule. Although the neo-Nazis did not support the existing government and used the excuse that democracy weakened the government through liberal traditions, the neo-Nazi responses to authority supported the concept of authoritarianism.

Last, the paranoia of communism that pervaded the West over the past 40 years led to a higher visibility for Marxist and Socialist movements than those on the right. The media carried the news associated with the Red Army Faction and the associated left-wing terrorist groups extensively over the past two decades. Only in the late 1980s did the media begin to accentuate the activities of the most obvious right-wing militant organizations, the neo-Nazis, although the most violent acts were perpetrated in the late 1970s and early 1980s.

Paul Wilkinson, a noted specialist of terrorism, provided an excellent evaluation of right-wing terrorism when he said that "fascist terrorism is not a sign of growing political strength, but a sign of frustration due to an inability to obtain power through politics."[8] When considering the neo-Nazis, this statement suggests reasons for their militancy. The neo-Nazis, by assuming many of the trappings of Hitler's Nazi organization and developing an extreme pro-German nationalist ideology, were forced to keep their activities clandestine during the first 30 years following World War II. The laws of West Germany following World War II made it almost impossible for a political organization to support any positions that were associated with the NSDAP during the 1930s and 1940s. Therefore, the evolution of a revised Nazism was suppressed during the first three decades following the war. Attempts at gaining a political foothold resulted in the banishment of the Socialist Reich Party, the premier postwar ultra-right organization that espoused portions of the past Nazi heritage. The NPD remained small and was continually forced to stay within the limits of legality with their continuing right-wing rhetoric. Politically, the far-right extremists were largely impotent during the 1950s, 1960s, and 1970s.

Not until the late 1970s and early 1980s did the militant fringe of the right wing become overtly active. The neo-Nazis, the most militant of the right wing, were on the fringes of the rightist parties for years, but until the late 1970s had remained secretive societies that remained incognito in order to stay out of the limelight of the German judicial system. However, by the late 1970s, younger leaders of these groups, such as Michael Kühnen, began to vocalize the neo-Nazi position. Initially, the frustrations of not being able to find a niche in the German political system led to actions that were considered criminal by the government and terrorist by others. Incidents of foreigners being killed, along with threats, and harassment against those opposing the neo-Nazi ideologies became far more frequent during the 1970s and 1980s. During the next five years, neo-Nazi militant activity became far more visible. However, the government's aggressive response was instrumental in severely limiting the potential threat posed by the neo-Nazis. The result was the beginning of these extremists actively participating in political elections during 1988 and 1989. The neo-Nazi support of right-wing candidates in Berlin and Frankfurt during the spring of 1989 showed that the ultra-right militants were capable of developing a limited political base. This was done by forming alliances with other right-wing groups. On the other hand, the neo-Nazis also showed that if they are unable to participate politically, that they are capable of using terrorism.

The major frustrations that seemed to prevail among the neo-Nazis were linked to their inability to coalesce into an effective mass movement. The primary problem appeared to be the inability of the divergent leadership of the many neo-Nazi organizations to combine their efforts and lead the rank and file membership into a common political force. The reason for this inability to effectively organize was the inherent problem of leadership that existed in the neo-Nazi structure. All of the ultra-right militant groups were predicated on the idea of authoritative leadership. Each group was led by a dominant leader who tended not to want to share leadership with anyone else. As long as this lack of unification existed, the neo-Nazis remained impotent as an individual viable political force. However, the frustration of not having any political power led these separate groups to activities that would gain attention for their individual programs. This often included the use of terrorism. The numbers of neo-Nazi members increased over the decade of the 1980s, and yet the leadership problems were not resolved.[9]

The primary targets for neo-Nazi terrorist activities over the past decade were foreigners. According to Hamburg State Minister of Interior Alfons Pawelczyk, as of the fall of 1986 the right-wing radicals (in this case primarily referring to neo-Nazi activities) were increasingly using violence against immigrants and asylum seekers from Third World countries.[10] Pawelczyk went on to say that outlawing such groups would be ineffective because "they would continue their dirty work in different organizational forms."[11]

Support for the neo-Nazi positions dealing with foreigners spread throughout Germany in the early 1980s. Over 70 percent of the population in Pawelczyk's region indicated that the laws dealing with asylum seekers were too liberal.[12] The neo-Nazis, playing on public opinion, developed a position that was popular with the majority of the population and yet overshadowed the deeper ramifications of the neo-Nazi beliefs.

Another of the specific targets that the neo-Nazis tradition-

ally attacked either verbally or physically were the forces stationed in West Germany under the auspices of the Western
defense alliance, NATO. Since 1981, the right-wing political
machines and the ultra-rightist neo-Nazis have expressed both
political and personal hostility against the U.S. and British
presence in West Germany. The neo-Nazis were found to have
been directly involved in the bombings of U.S. servicemen's
vehicles in Buzbach, Darmstadt, and Frankfurt during December 1981, which injured one Army soldier. Up until this blatant
terrorist action, the right wing had repeatedly argued that the
European military were too dependent upon NATO, especially
the United States. They said that this dependency generally
threatened the sovereignty, national culture, and mode of existence of Europeans.[13] The neo-Nazis accepted this right-wing
position as a primary goal to pursue.

In addition to the quest for German nationalism, which excludes foreigners and foreign military presence, the neo-Nazis
placed themselves into the traditional role of protector against
communism and as the supporters of racial purity. However,
although they were adamantly opposed to communism, the neo-
Nazis conducted no specific incidents of terrorism against Socialist or Communist targets. The primary efforts throughout
the 1980s were directed against foreigners, thereby insuring
that the neo-Nazi programs were not endangered by a radical
resurgence of anti-Nazi public opinion.

What types of people were drawn to the terrorist neo-Nazi
organizations? Where were the most militant elements located?
What types of terrorist activities were associated with this
militant right-wing culture? In looking at Table 5.1 it is evident
that as of 1981 the dominate neo-Nazi terrorist activities were
centered in the northern regions of West Germany. Hamburg
and Kiel led the West German states in numbers of right-wing
terrorists. This did not necessarily mean that the other states
were exempt from terrorism. This table also indicates that out
of the respondents that the government appointed researchers
interviewed, the majority who identified themselves as terrorists lived in the north. In the case of this particular query, 52
percent refused to answer, therefore making the final estimate
suspect. What is apparent from those who did respond was that

Table 5.1
1981 Locations of Right-Wing Terrorists

CITY TERRORISTS	RIGHT-WING	LEFT-WING TERRORISTS
Hamburg	22%	25%
Kiel	13%	2%
West Berlin	9%	42%
Düsseldorf	4%	4%
Bonn	4%	4%
Stuttgart	4%	10%

Source: Jäger et al, <u>Lebenslaufanalyses</u>, 69. Note: Only 48% of those right-wing militants that were questioned responded to this particular question. The balance of the respondents were from other cities within West Germany. The percentages were too small to include on the table.

an active radical neo-Nazi influence existed in West Germany. It is also evident that northern Germany harbored a fair number of these modern Nazis.

Between 1978 and 1985, the types of acts perpetrated by the neo-Nazi activists included: 28 murders, 20 bombings, 77 cases of arson, 14 robberies, 208 assaults, and 310 incidents of criminal damage.[14] In addition, neo-Nazis were identified as the culprits in approximately 1,216 cases of threatening people and over 11,829 incidents of breaking federal and state laws during this same seven year period.[15] What is apparent from these statistics is that the neo-Nazis relied on threats and petty criminal efforts to obtain notoriety and to wield influence on a localized level. This did not preclude some of the more extremist members from committing far more spectacular terrorist actions, such as murder, bombing, and arson.

Table 5.2 shows the breakdown of types of punishable acts that were accomplished by the neo-Nazi elements from the mid-1970s to 1981. Although only 65 percent of the respondents answered this query, those who did, and those who considered themselves terrorists, identified the types of activities that were conducted by members of the neo-Nazi affiliated groups. These were then compared to the activities associated with the

Table 5.2
Types of Punishable Acts

Acts	Right-wing	Left-wing
Participated in a Criminal Association	52%	73%
Assisted in a Criminal Association	0%	34%
Formed a Criminal Association	17%	26%
Unauthorized Weapon Possession	26%	52%
False Documents	4%	39%
Theft	13%	29%
Murder	13%	33%
Bombing	9%	32%
Hostage Taking	0%	16%
Serious Injury	13%	10%
Resistance to Arrest	4%	26%
Serious Robbery	9%	27%

Source: Jäger et al, Lebenslaufanalyses, 62.

radical left, whose respondents identified themselves as primarily members of the Red Army Faction (RAF).

Neo-Nazi groups, dominated in the 1980s by the conservative youth, tended to become involved in fewer acts of violence than their left-wing counterparts, but often the results were more spectacular in the numbers of injuries and deaths. This was evidenced by the bombing at the Munich *Oktoberfest* in 1980 and in the attacks against foreigners who individually were not considered targets, but collectively provided a potential target of terrorist opportunity.

The right-wing neo-Nazis did not develop a sustained program of terrorism during the 1980s. However, when terrorism was used, their attacks were often aimed at general, rather than selective targets. Although not random or unplanned, these attacks were mostly made against refugee and immigrant-worker housing, which indiscriminately killed and injured a large number of people. These types of attacks were often far less sophisticated than the attacks made by the leftist extremists. Left-wing terrorists developed fairly sophisticated methods of bomb making, attacks, and use of modern weapons during the 1970s and 1980s.

Neo-Nazi militant groups that were involved in terrorist types of activities during the 1980s were organized into cellular units. This was a popular method that most terrorist organizations used to insure security. The neo-Nazi groups revolved around the clique arrangement where members were chosen to join and became close knit under the leadership of one primary leader. This comradeship was extremely important in obtaining members, primarily because many missed this security and bonding in their individual family or professional environments.

The actual numbers of active, strict neo-Nazis have been difficult to ascertain. In 1983, estimates were provided by specialists in terrorism that indicated that there were about 1,000 strict neo-Nazi adherents that could be potentially dangerous as terrorists.[16] In addition, most sources have suggested that approximately 20,000 sympathizers exist that would support potential actions by the "hardcore" members. The West Berlin Jewish leader, Heinz Galinski, suggested that there were from 22,100 to 23,000 active supporters of neo-Nazism in West Germany, 230 of which he considered militant.[17] Both the West German Interior Minister and the SPD leadership have estimated numbers of active neo-Nazis at between 1,500 and 2,100, and that there were approximately 25,000 right-wing supporters as of 1987.[18] These numbers indicate a potential terrorist capability that is four times greater than the highly publicized Red Army Faction (RAF) of the left-wing German extremists. This potential has not been released to any great degree, but continues to fester on the fringes of German society.

NEO-NAZI TERRORISM

The appearance of neo-Nazi terrorism in Germany was sobering to much of the population. The previous clandestine activities of these radical groups were traditionally limited to outbursts of Nazi propaganda and attempts to use threats and bombast to place themselves in the public eye. However, the most militant groups in the 1980s brought out a far more radical and aggressive manner that was reminiscent of Hitler's SA brownshirt paramilitary methods.

In the 1970s, neo-Nazi activities began to show evidence of future violent actions. A militant group called *Aktion Wider-*

Table 5.3
Right-Wing Extremists and Neo-Nazi Offenses, 1976–1980

	1974	1975	1976	1977	1978	1979	1980
Total Offenses	136	206	319	616	992	1483	1643
Violent Acts*	22	21	16	40	52	97	113
Convictions			34	46	150	365	NA
Investigations			80	317	610	836	876
Police Searches				60	141	221	267

Source: Baeyer-Katte et al, Gruppenprozesse, 444.
*Between 1983 and 1987 there were 388 violent acts documented, plus 29 terrorist acts
and 762 violent threats.

stand launched a campaign against the West German governmental program, *Ostpolitik*, which provided the basis for a
closer relationship with East Germany. Inherent in this policy
were the recognition and sense of detente with Communist
neighbors. This led to the right-wing militants losing faith in
the political means and moving away from the NPD, which
was becoming emasculated. A revival of anti-Semitism, and a
more visible physical presence that incorporated the use of
uniforms and other military paraphernalia, heralded the coming of a more radicalized neo-Nazi movement. West German
police began to uncover caches of weapons, explosives, and ammunition. In February 1978, investigations into the burglary
of a Dutch bivouac, located in West Germany's state of Lower
Saxony, showed that four machine guns had been stolen.[19] Police traced the burglary to a group in which a number of the
members were identified as neo-Nazis. In the same year, the
West German police also uncovered a cache of arms totalling
230 firearms, plus explosives and bombs, that were directly
linked to neo-Nazi terrorists.[20]

Terrorist-related actions that were attributed to right-wing
militants showed a steady increase from 1976 through 1980
(see Table 5.3).[21] From 1983 to 1987, the West German government identified 29 instances of terrorism that were conducted by neo-Nazis.[22] In addition, members of these same
groups perpetrated 388 violent acts and 762 threats of violence.[23] From 1978 to 1988, there were 25 deaths attributed to

neo-Nazi terrorist acts.[24] These included the 1980 deaths of two Vietnamese students in a youth hostel in Hamburg, which were blamed on members of Manfred Roeder's neo-Nazi group, *Deutsche Aktionsgruppen*.

Frank Schubert, a known neo-Nazi, shot and killed a border guard at the Swiss-German border in 1980. Schubert was attempting to smuggle a weapon and ammunition into West Germany. After killing the policeman, Schubert then committed suicide. In 1981, the neo-Nazi, Friedhelm Enk, murdered Johannes Bügner who was suspected of supplying information to local police about the group's activities and membership and of being homosexual. Enk was thought to have been selected by the leadership of his organization to eliminate Bügner. One year later in 1982, the professed neo-Nazi, Helmut Oxner, shot two black Americans and an Egyptian, thinking they were Turks. Following the shooting, Oxner was killed by police in a shootout.

Neo-Nazi terrorists continued to target Turkish immigrants into the mid-1980s. Neo-Nazi affiliated skinheads were found to have been involved in the brutal murder of a Turk by the name of Kaymakei. In July 1985, these militant neo-Nazis who were adamantly against foreigners, particularly the Turks, were looking for a victim. Kaymakei was a convenient target and was killed with, what it appeared at the time, little remorse. Later, this same group of skinheads killed another Turk and his friend in Hamburg.

These deaths were all attributed to the basic antiforeign ideology that permeated the most militant neo-Nazi organizations. The total numbers of individual incidents do not indicate the full extent of the terrorism that these groups perpetrated. Violent acts, threats, and demonstrations of power became more prevalent throughout the 1980s. Even with the temporary loss of leaders through imprisonment, neo-Nazi activities continued.

The death of Rudolf Hess in 1987 provided an event that offered the opportunity for the right wing to show their strength. Hess, one of Hitler's deputies, was sentenced to life imprisonment during the Nuremberg trials following the war. He died at the age of 93 from an apparent suicide. Hess was found in his cell choked to death with an electrical cord. There were doubts raised, particularly by Hess's son, as to whether it was suicide or was perpetrated by the Allies in order to finally close the chapter on the last remaining incarcerated Nazi leader. His death stirred the neo-Nazis into a visible reaction. Small, but vocal, demonstrations were held outside the Spandau Prison, where Hess had spent the past 43 years, and in the area of his burial site in Wunsiedel, West Germany. The old and still familiar "Sieg Heil" was chanted by the neo-Nazis in remembrance of the Nazi past. Fears by many of the West German population that the death and burial of such a noted Nazi would result in violence were unfounded since the right-wing extremist activity dwindled soon after the announcement of the death. However, isolated incidents did occur that showed the potential of the neo-Nazi extremism. Three days after the death of Hess, the Frankfurt police arrested two neo-Nazis who had planted a bomb in a local train station, but which proved to be a dud. Two days after the bombing attempt, a supposed neo-Nazi member threw a firebomb at the offices of the SPD youth organization headquarters in Duesseldorf and wrote "revenge for Hess" on the Berlin Wall.[25]

West German officials conducted a search of nearly 1,000 suspected neo-Nazi residences on 24 March 1981.[26] This search was designed to find the sources of large amounts of Nazi propaganda that was beginning to surface throughout West Germany. The results of this sweep were of special interest to the German government. Large quantities of published material were found that had been imported from the United States and Canada. The majority of this material originated in Lincoln, Nebraska and was traced to a U.S. group called the NSDAP-*Auslands und Aufbauorganisation* (NSDAP-AO). This U.S. neo-Nazi organization was led by Gary Rex Lauck and was the primary source of neo-Nazi materials being distributed throughout Europe. Titles of these materials included: "Foreigners Out," "Down with the Red Front," and "Do Not Buy From Jews," along with numerous small publications against Jews, blacks, Asians, and so-called "half-breeds."[27] In addition to these propaganda materials, the sweep uncovered revolvers, rifles, and ammunition that were being collected and stored in a number of separate residences and safehouses.

The first neo-Nazi terrorist actions of consequence began in 1980. Prior to this year, the majority of activities from these radicals involved threats and arson. By early 1980, the more violent neo-Nazi groups began using terrorism as a tool. German State Police arrested six neo-Nazis, of the then active Kexel-Hepp organization, during an attempted bank robbery in early 1980.[28]

Members of the same group, upon being interrogated, revealed that they were involved in the bombing of U.S. servicemen's cars in Darmstadt earlier that year, which resulted in injury to an American soldier.[29] This incident was only the beginning of the infamous year of 1980, known for the number of terrorist acts perpetrated by neo-Nazis throughout Germany.

On 21 August 1980, members of the now outlawed *Deutsche Aktionsgruppe*, an extremely violent antiforeigner organization, placed a bomb in a boardinghouse for foreigners in Hamburg. The bomb killed two Vietnamese students. A month later, on 26 September 1980, at the famous Munich *Oktoberfest*, Gundolf Köhler attempted to place a bomb, made of 24 pounds of high explosives, at the entrance of the Munich festival area. The bomb prematurely exploded killing Köhler and 12 others.[30] An additional 200 were injured, 72 of them critically.[31] Initially, the police viewed Köhler as a lone criminal, who, although he was identified as a neo-Nazi, was considered to have planned and executed the bombing on his own. After extensive investigation, it became apparent that Köhler was a part of the Hoffman group, an extremely active and militant neo-Nazi organization. The investigators speculated that Köhler placed the bomb on the instructions of his group leader, Karl Heinz Hoffman, an avowed neo-Nazi and the organizer of the *Wehrsportgruppen Hoffman*. West German government officials argued that the Munich *Oktoberfest* bombing was a "copy cat" attempt of the bombing of the Bologna train station in Italy, which was perpetrated by Italian neo-fascists.[32]

Hoffman's group surfaced again in December 1980, when a member was connected with the murder of the Jewish publisher, Shlomo Pevin and his close friend, Mrs. Frieda Pöschke. The investigation revealed that Vive Behrendt, a *Wehrsport-gruppen Hoffman* member, committed the murder on the orders of the group leader, Karl Hoffman. Behrendt took refuge in an Arab Al Fatah training camp in the Middle East and therefore was out of the immediate jurisdiction of the West German authorities.

The early attacks that the right-wing militants conducted were examples of fairly unsophisticated terrorist methods. This indicated that the neo-Nazis were not necessarily familiar with the sophisticated use of terror. Errors in judgment, such as the premature explosion at the *Oktoberfest*, and poorly planned assassination attempts, led the police to the perpetrators. The naiveté shown by the early neo-Nazi efforts of using terrorism as a weapon was quite obvious after evaluating the difference between rightist terrorists and leftist terrorists in West Germany during the same period in 1980. The leftists developed a more advanced and sophisticated technique of terrorism over the previous decade. They were after specific targets that gained them the most notoriety and provided the greatest usable response from the media and the government. These terrorists, particularly the Red Army Faction, took great care in planning and executing their acts of violence. On the other hand, the neo-Nazis tended to attract attention through the killing of large numbers of people, rather than specific targets. Both ideological groups wanted the attention that caused despair and fear among specific target audiences. However, the neo-Nazis's methods were also designed to cause maximum social disorder, which could potentially provide an opportunity for an authoritarian takeover. Over 108 violent incidents were attributed to neo-Nazis in 1981. By 1982, the numbers of incidents had dropped to 64, but each action was far more violent than those of the previous year.[33]

The increase in violence was exemplified when neo-Nazis murdered three foreigners in Nuremberg and three attempts were made to murder U.S. soldiers in the Rhineland, all of which failed. The neo-Nazis's use of threats of violence rose from 197 in 1981 to 241 in 1982.[34] Neo-Nazi violence, and the increasing use of threats, drew the attention of the West Germans to the apparent revival of radical right-wing extremism in West Germany. No longer were the militant members restrained by memories of Hitler's Germany, the ravages of war, or the weakly enforced laws against Nazism.

MILITANT ORGANIZATIONS

Although there were a number of right-wing radical organizations that came and went over the four decades following World War II, there were relatively few that became so extreme as to use terrorist methods. Even among the most radical of the right wing, the neo-Nazis, those who resorted to terrorism were limited. However, the more modern neo-Nazi groups continued to provide a virulent and antidemocratic stance that often resulted in violence. At the end of the 1970s, following the almost total dissolution of the NPD, two terrorist neo-Nazi groups emerged. These two groups were the *Wehrsportgruppen Hoffman* and *Deutsche Aktionsgruppe*. Between them the members of these groups spearheaded the rising neo-Nazi extremism in West Germany. They were responsible for eight bombings and arson attacks, 24 desecrations of Jewish cemeteries, and 41 additional acts of violence and vandalism in a one year period.[35]

Manfred Roeder, a lawyer who was born in 1930, was the leader of the *Deutsche Aktionsgruppe* (DA). Roeder's activities as a neo-Nazi were extensive. He traveled outside of Germany gathering support and was vehemently against the Allied occupation of Germany and the existing West German government. Roeder was arrested in 1978 and jailed for incitement. He was arrested again in 1980, at which time he was sentenced to 13 years, the term to begin in June 1982. This sentence was for his implied involvement in the bombing of the youth hostel in Hamburg in 1980, resulting in the deaths of two young Vietnamese. Two of Roeder's colleagues, Raymond Hörnle and Sybille Vorderbrugge, were the actual participants in the bombing. They were also arrested and convicted, each receiving a sentence of life imprisonment. The two were members of Roeder's *Deutsche Aktionsgruppe*.

Karl Heinz Hoffman, a young man who was apparently in-

trigued with military equipment and activities, organized and
led *Wehrsportgruppen Hoffman*. Originally, the Hoffman group
contented themselves with "playing" soldier in the forested
areas around the Nuremberg region and on Hoffman's small
estate. However, by 1980, the group became rabidly anti-
Semitic and strongly nationalist. Their exploits into terrorism
during 1980 culminated in the dissolution of the group, as many
of the members were caught and tried for crimes within Germany. In late 1980, the West German government outlawed
the organization, forcing many of its remaining members to
leave Germany and seek refuge in adjacent countries and in
Lebanon.

An early neo-Nazi group that showed little regard for the
law and was defiantly Nazi oriented was the *Aktionsgemeinschaft Nationaler Sozialisten*-ANS (National Socialist Common Action Group). Michael Kühnen formed the ANS in
1977. This group carried out a number of arms thefts and
robberies in the late 1970s, before the police broke the organization. Michael Kühnen was arrested in 1978 and his
henchman, Christian Worch, assumed the group's leadership
until he was arrested in 1980 for participating in a number
of bombings. The result of the group losing two leaders and
the governmental banning of the organization was the dissolution of the formal membership.

Kühnen, however, was not to be denied his future as a premier leader of the radical neo-Nazis in Germany. Time and
again he showed the ability to bounce back from the government's efforts to eliminate neo-Nazi influences. After being
arrested in 1978 and spending a short period in prison, Kühnen
traveled to Paris, France, where he remained out of reach of
the German authorities while continuing his efforts to organize
yet another neo-Nazi organization. Once again, his new organization, *Aktionsgemeinschaft Nationaler Sozialisten-
Nationale Aktivisten* was banned in Germany in December
1983. Kühnen was brought to trial in January 1985 and sentenced to three years and four months for illegally disseminating neo-Nazi propaganda.[36]

Although facing a prison term, Kühnen simply renamed the
banned ANS-NA organization and continued to attract mem-

bers. Between 1985 and 1989, this spinoff of the ANS-NA, referred to as "The Movement," began developing a membership of neo-Nazis that was largely under Kühnen's influence, although he was incarcerated. This organization picked up where the banned group left off in 1983. The primary goal of the newly developed organization was to renew the NSDAP Party in Germany.[37] Kühnen's position was made quite clear in early 1989 as he suggested to journalists from the German magazine *Der Spiegel* that, "our dream is a race of European SA, that is active as political soldiers of National Socialism that fight in the streets and overcome the perceived enemies and organizations."[38]

"The Movement" carried forward the old programs initiated by Kühnen in the original ANS-NA organization. But in 1986 a split occurred within the new organization. Some of Kühnen's followers went on to reorganize into the more politically oriented *Nationale Sammlung*-NS, which translated means "National Gathering." The other wing remained more traditional neo-Nazi, retaining less visibility to the outside and continuing the more militant means of gaining attention. This splinter group came under the leadership of Jürgen Mosler and Volker Heidel.

By late 1988 and early 1989, Kühnen, having been released from prison, became more actively involved in a right-wing movement to gain political positions in local elections rather than to pursue terrorist activities. The government, fearing the apparent right-wing political strength, once again found it necessary to ban Kühnen's neo-Nazi organization. Four weeks before the Hesse elections, Bundesminister Friedrich Zimmerman (CSU) banned the *Nationale Sammlung*. The banning was based on the NS electioneering for the establishment of "foreign free towns" within West Germany. This, of course, was reminiscent of the *"Judenfreie"* towns that were developed under Hitler. Kühnen's outspokenness about his desires to reinstate the NSDAP, and to use Hitler as a model, only fueled the government's desire to suppress the neo-Nazis. Police raided 40 homes of suspected neo-Nazis in six of the states of West Germany. As a result of the raids, officials found pictures of Hitler, swastikas, and propaganda materials. In Kühnen's residence in Frankfurt, officials found a box of ammunition, along with Nazi memorabilia and propaganda.

Although Kühnen's organization was banned, he immediately declared a new neo-Nazi group that he claimed would continue to fight for right-wing ideology. Assuming the new name "Initiative of the People's Will," many of the members of the banned NS moved forward with efforts to incorporate neo-Nazi ideas into modern German politics.

The one-hundredth birthday of Adolf Hitler proved to be another opportunity for Michael Kühnen to express his neo-Nazism to Europe. Hitler's birthday, 20 April 1989, was planned as a day of recognition among the European neo-Nazis, led by Kühnen and the venerable old Nazi, Leon Dagrelle, who, at the age of 82 experienced a lifelong dream.[39] He was the honorary president of the European Hitler Commemorative Organization, which was responsible for the arrangements for Hitler's birthday celebration. Dagrelle was the highest foreign director involved, since he was identified as the deputy "Fuhrer" of the Belgium SS-Freiwilligen-Legion, a strong neo-Nazi group within Belgium.

Between Kühnen and Dagrelle, the birthday party for Hitler drew together neo-Nazi groups from within Germany and throughout Europe. Countries represented were Spain, France, Denmark, Belgium, Norway, and West Germany.[40] This event showed the extent in which Kühnen had gained a reputation among fellow neo-Nazis as a leader of some circumstance.

Although Michael Kühnen was the most verbal and obvious supporter of neo-Nazism over the past ten years, other organizations with similar tendencies toward violence and threats prevailed as well. An organization that evolved following the banning of Kühnen's ANS-NA was the *Freie Arbeiter Partei*. Led by Heinz Gero Reiss, formerly the ideological leader for the *Nationale Sammlung*, this group was considered to be the new political arm of the neo-Nazis. Their emphasis was away from threats and acts of overt violence and was turned toward political power. Their methods were effective in insuring a win for right-wing candidates in the 1989 Frankfurt elections and their efforts have borne fruit in the Rhine-Westphalia region. Kühnen, himself, threw his support towards the *Freie Arbeiter*

Partei in the early 1989 elections, as was evidenced by his comments in March 1989 when he said, "there (Rhine-Westphalia) they would prove that National Socialism will be won back city by city and area by area."[41]

The *Freiheitliche Deutsche Arbeiterpartei* (FAP) boasted the largest active membership of the radical neo-Nazi groups in early 1989 with over 500 members. This organization is still located primarily in the North Rhineland-Westphalia region, where about 180 active known members reside. The majority of the identified members in this region live in Hamburg, Hessen, Niedersachenn, Bremen, and Baden-Wurttenberg.[42] Other smaller groupings of members live in Bavaria and Schleswig-Holstein, although numerically they were far fewer than in the north central region of West Germany. The impact of the size of the organization was shown throughout the election campaign as groups marched in Dortmund, Witten, Hamburg, Bonn, and Duisberg.[43]

Referred to as the "political" neo-Nazi organization by many journalists and the Bonn government, the FAP became the most active right-wing neo-Nazi extremist group to participate in the 1989 German elections. Because of the less militant approach to spreading neo-Nazi ideology, this group has experienced splintering of their more militant factions. The government officials became aware of these more militant neo-Nazis after arresting a leader of the FAP, Siegfried Müller, in 1986 for arson. During interrogation, Müller identified Bernd Futter, a 30 year-old militant neo-Nazi, as the key individual responsible for the arson attacks. Futter was found to be the leader of an extremely rabid neo-Nazi group that espoused the use of terrorism to gain attention. This organization was called the "Sport and Security Comradeship of the Iron Cross First Class," a group that had broken away from the main FAP element because the FAP was "too slack."[44] Bernd Futter was found guilty of four cases of arson which included a Turkish translation agency, a home occupied by foreigners, a house occupied by people considered by Futter to be Communists, and a police station.

In another case, a separate splinter group from the FAP, known as EK-1, was identified by government officials when four members of the Hanover group were arrested for murdering a comrade. The group thought that the person they murdered was a police informer. The four EK-1 members were between 18 and 19 years of age and the victim was 17. The death of the youth was caused by beating and was thought to have been done by orders from leaders within the EK-1 organization.[45] Police believed that the EK-1 was responsible for at least four arson attacks, an armed robbery, and burglary of a West German weapons manufacturer.

Although the FAP was not subjected to a ban by the Minister of the Interior, the group continued to provide a central neo-Nazi organization which had extreme radical militants either directly or indirectly associated. The political fortunes of the FAP improved dramatically in West Germany, primarily due to the intense feelings about foreigners and asylum seekers that were unleashed in 1988 and early 1989. The approximately 500 active members generated a reasonable political following that drew support from other neo-Nazi and right-wing extremist groups during the most recent elections in 1989 and 1990.

In addition to the larger, more visible neo-Nazi groups such as FAP and the ever-changing named organizations that Michael Kühnen led, there are other small organizations as shown in Table 5.4 that continued to revolve around the fringes of Germany's right wing. For example, the *Hilfsorganisation für Nationale Politische Gefangene und deren Angehörige e.V.* (HNG) is an extremely small group, having dropped from 21 known members to 16 between January 1987 and November 1987. This particular group, although small and apparently inconsequential, carried a reputation for extreme militancy and was directly supported by Michael Kühnen's "The Movement."

The *Nationalistische Front* (NF) was fairly active during the mid-1980s in supporting anti-Zionist programs. This group was led by Manhof Schönbonn and boasted a total of 80 active members in 1985. This particular organization supported a national revolution that included both cultural and social changes within Germany. This was an offshoot of a neo-Nazi ideology that was different from that attributed to the hard-core groups that supported Kühnen. Referred to as "National Revolution-

Table 5.4
Identified Neo-Nazi Organizations in 1987

Organization	Members
Arbeitsgemeinschaft Nationaler Verbände/Völkischer Bund (ANV/VB) (Wiesbaden)	25
Bürger-und Bauerninitiative e.V. (BBI) (Hannover)	100
Deutsche Bürgerinitiative e.V. (DBI) (Schwarzenborn/Knüll)	120
Committee for the Celebration of Hitler's Birthday (Kühnen's & Mosler's Groups)	500
Freiheitliche Deutsche Arbeiterpartei (FAP)	500
Hilfsorganisation für Nationale Politische Gefangene und deren Angehörige e.V. (HNG) (Frankfurt)	220
Nationalistische Front (NF) (Bielefeld)	80
Neonazikreis um Curt Müller (Mainz)	not available
Neonazizentrum Ernst Tag	not available
NSDAP-Auslands und Aufbauorganisation (NSDAP-OA) (United States)	not available

Source: Bundesminister des Innern, Verfassungsschutzbericht(1987), 131-132.

ary Neo-Nazis" by the federal government, these groups, which included the *Nationalistische Front* (NF), were considered followers of the two brothers, Dr. Otto Strasser and Gregor Strasser. The Strasser brothers provided a socialist flare to the National Socialists during the formative years prior to Hitler's accession to power. Hitler eliminated these opponents to his brand of politics at the first viable opportunity, thereby squelching any anticipated efforts to incorporate socialist ideas into Nazi ideology. These groups, therefore, had a major difference in ideology, which led to support for some socialist concepts.[46] This, however, did not preclude these organizations from pursuing neo-Nazi activities and having similar nationalist goals.

Another rather virulent neo-Nazi group was known as *Arbeitsgemeinschaft Nationaler Verbände/Völkischer Bund* (ANV/VB). This organization was begun in March 1987 by Peter Naumann under the motto "Kampf den Dunkelmannern" (Fight the Black Man).[47] The primary targets were NATO and U.S. personnel. After 1987, this group showed a tendency to develop international connections, particularly with neo-Nazi groups in the United States and in northern Europe.

There were other very small, but yet locally visible neo-Nazi groups throughout West Germany during the 1980s. These groups included such neo-Nazi militant organizations as Curt and Ursala Müller's local neo-Nazis; *Bürger und Bauerninitiative e.V.* (BBI), led by Theis Christophersen, age 69; and the *Deutsche Bürgerinitiative e.V.* (DBI), led by Manfred Roeder's wife, Gertraud Roeder. These groups were not linked to specific cases of terrorism, but have been vocal in their locales in subjecting the local populations to neo-Nazi propaganda.

The neo-Nazi's were organized into 20 groups during the early 1980s. Out of a total of 69 identified right-wing extremist organizations, totalling over 25,000 active adherents, the neo-Nazis only numbered about 1,400, yet proved to be aggressive and were linked to a number of terrorist activities throughout the early 1980s. A number of skinheads were included in the neo-Nazi ranks. In 1984, the NPD used some of these skinheads, who were considered excessively militant, as protection troops.[48] This arrangement proved to be short-lived due to the lack of control that could be maintained with these types of right-wing radicals. The total skinhead population in West Germany was estimated in 1988 to be about 2,500. Only 10 percent were known to have joined with the right-wing extremists, and normally with neo-Nazi groups such as the FAP.[49] Their inclusion in these neo-Nazi groups tended to raise the level of militancy and led to more aggressive violent acts, often at local sports events.

GOVERNMENT RESPONSES TO NEO-NAZISM

By early 1980, the West German government was intimately aware of the growing militancy of the right-wing neo-Nazis. Information gathered from members, who were arrested for numerous types of illegal activities, portrayed the neo-Nazis as extreme radicals, many of whom had resorted to terrorist tactics. Police and justice officials normally viewed these militants as common criminals and prosecuted them under criminal laws, rather than under the specific laws associated with terrorism. The results were often fairly short sentences. Otfried Hepp, a neo-Nazi from Frankfurt, who was extradited from France, was sentenced in 1986 to ten and one-half years for attempted murder, being a member of a terrorist group, using explosives, and being involved in four bank robberies.[50] Hepp was identified in the trial as a leading neo-Nazi in a Frankfurt organization. This particular group was rabidly anti-American and was involved in a car-bombing incident against American servicemen in 1982. As was the case in many of the neo-Nazi arrests and trials during the 1980s, Hepp confessed to his involvement with the neo-Nazis, and then offered the German police inside information on the extent of neo-Nazism in the Frankfurt region.

Police efforts continued to net neo-Nazi weapons caches and identify militant membership during the mid-1980s. A police raid on a designated neo-Nazi camp was conducted in the late spring of 1987. This camp was located outside of a small German community where the neo-Nazis planned to hold an illegal demonstration. The result was the arrest of 19 neo-Nazi members who were armed with guns, knives, and clubs. In addition to the arrests, police found additional arms, posters of Hitler and other Nazi paraphernalia, all of which were banned in West Germany.

Key neo-Nazi leaders were arrested and sentenced to varying lengths of prison terms throughout the early 1980s in an attempt to suppress the neo-Nazi movement. In January 1985, Michael Kühnen, the self-appointed successor to Hitler, was sentenced to three years and four months for distributing banned propaganda. As mentioned earlier, he remained active in the neo-Nazi movement and, upon release, was directly influential in the success of right-wing extremists running as candidates under the auspices of the NPD during the February-March 1989 elections in Frankfurt.

Government fears that the burial of Rudolf Hess would result in a general demonstration by the right-wing were assuaged through the use of the low-key police procedures. The governmental actions taken included such approaches as a low profile movement from West Berlin to the burial location and a private family burial that remained under tight security. These methods of retaining strict control resulted in minimal publicity and inhibited any major confrontations with the Hess supporters.

For the most part, the Federal Republic judicial system meted out prison terms to those who were found guilty of the most violent crimes. Between 1982 and 1987, 13 neo-Nazis were imprisoned for between eight years and life. The accused neo-Nazi, Hörnle, who had placed the bomb that killed the two Vietnamese, was sentence to life in prison. Kexel, convicted of placing the bombs in American servicemen's automobiles in 1982, was sentenced to 14 years. A key neo-Nazi, Manfred Roeder, was sentenced to 13 years in 1982 for his involvement as a leader of a suspected terrorist group, *Deutsche Aktionsgruppen.*

The apparent move toward terrorism by the more militant neo-Nazis was accentuated by the types of weapons and munitions found during police raids. Between 1985 and 1987, officials found 120 guns and machine guns and over 12,000 rounds of ammunition.[51] In addition, there were about 150 knives and clubs, along with ample materials to make bombs and explosives.[52] In early 1989, Michael Kühnen's followers were subjected to a police raid, resulting in additional findings of arms, ammunition, and Nazi propaganda. These raids made the West German officials even more cognizant of the potential threat that could evolve from the neo-Nazis.

Police and government attempts to control the terrorist activities within West Germany showed great progress throughout the 1980s. Cooperation with other countries and development of more stringent controls proved to be effective against both left-wing and right-wing extremists.

The North Atlantic Treaty Organization (NATO) supported regional European police efforts by setting up an information exchange service about international terrorists. Another police structure that evolved was TREVI (Terrorism, Radicalism, & Violence International). Members of this group track terrorists and represent the European Economic Community, Australia, Japan, and Switzerland.[53]

The West Germans developed a special computer storage facility in Wiesbaden, West Germany. Called "kommissar" by some, this system maintains all information about known terrorists and their supporters. The information bank includes such information as personal habits, interests and aliases, as well as definitive information about known safehouses and supporters. Although begun in response to the terrorist acts of the Red Army Faction, this facility provided an extensive array of information that was invaluable in obtaining a semblance of control over a rapidly expanding threat of European terrorism.

As early as 1977, Chancellor Willi Brandt warned that the German government would take action against "Nazi elements."[54] Actions taken included the banning of over 50 neo-Nazi publications from 1978 to 1979. For over 30 years, the neo-Nazis and right-wing extremists clandestinely grew in numbers and developed a following among a small portion of the German youth.

THE LAW AND EXTREMISM

Until late 1988, neo-Nazis were not normally classified as terrorists by the government. The West German government finally classified the right-wing extremists and left-wing extremists under the same laws in November 1988 in order to set a precedence for all extremism in the Federal Republic. There were a number of questions that were asked by the German judicial system when determining whether an organization could be classified as terrorist. Is it a terrorist association, as identified by the police and government? Are the members, themselves, identified formally as terrorists? Does the group plan and execute terrorist acts? For many years, West German government officials assumed that left-wing extremist groups met these standards.[55] The right wing, and in particular, neo-Nazis, were normally viewed as individual criminals that had overstepped the bounds of law in their efforts to further their ideology. There was, therefore, a tendency by government officials to assume that the groups themselves did not meet the criteria for being identified as terrorist. The result of this dichotomy was a difference in punishments for similar types of terrorist actions. Affiliation with a terrorist association (i.e., RAF), as determined by the government, called for far more stringent judicial responses. On the contrary, those groups, generally right-wing, that were identified as being made up of radical membership, usually received considerably lesser sentences and fines.[56] Therefore, neo-Nazi groups were not normally classified as terrorist associations and offenses were often ascribed to loners or were considered individual efforts.[57]

When the terrorist acts of both right and left are compared, there were some striking similarities. Each executed one of their own members for supposed treachery. Methods and targets were often the same, although the leftists appeared more sophisticated in their planning and execution of violent acts, as well as their abilities to develop weapons, most often bombs. Like the Red Army Faction, the neo-Nazis attempted to strike at Americans, particularly military. They traditionally viewed security personnel as serving an illegal West German government. The right-wing, supported by the most militant, embraced a nationalist environmentalism that sought racial purity of the German people and Germany. This concept was most effective in raising fears throughout West Germany about the influence of foreigners, particularly Turks, on the quality of German society. The last, and very important, similarity to the "terrorists" of the left, were the contacts with the Palestinians. Both the neo-Nazis and the Red Army Faction members participated in training camps in the Middle East. These camps were specifically designed to prepare these extremists for terrorist activities.

In looking at these distinct similarities, the differences between neo-Nazi "radicals" and RAF "terrorists" are more difficult to ascertain. In contrast, the right-wing militants emphasized that foreigners, both workers and asylum seekers, were interlopers in German society. Another difference was the reemergence of anti-Semitism among many of the neo-Nazis. The West German government reappraised the differences in late 1988 and concluded that both the right-wing extremists and the left-wing radicals were a similar threat and were to be dealt with in the same manner.

Many specialists in terrorism and modern historians of Germany consider the neo-Nazis as less of a threat than the left wing. Many of these opinions were developed during the quiescent period of neo-Nazism and the erosion of the right-wing political fortunes. It is interesting to note that the prognosis for an escalation of neo-Nazism was extremely limited during the latter 1970s and early 1980s. This corresponds with the attitudes of the West German government, which saw the neo-Nazis as a minimal threat.

Kurt Tauber provided one of the most definitive discussions of right-wing evolution in post-war Germany from 1945 to 1965 in his book, *Beyond Eagle and Swastika*. In his conclusions, Tauber commented that "neo-Nazism, in the sense of a political movement, is condemned to failure."[58] However, he went on to say that "radical nationalism and anti-liberal/anti-democratic authoritarianism were still vital ideological and political forces."[59] Tauber's conclusions identified a nationalist force that continued for two decades after the publication of his study and ultimately led to a limited revival of Nazism. The late 1970s and 1980s showed a revitalization of the ideology of the NSDAP through a new generation of neo-Nazis led by such men as Manfred Roeder, Michael Kühnen and, although for only a short time, Karl Heinz Hoffman.

Abraham Ashkenasi, writing in 1976, argued that the extreme nationalism that led to the NSDAP in the 1930s was dead "due to the defeat in war and a realization among the general population that extreme nationalism was evil."[60] Once again, the siren song of nationalism was apparent during the late 1980s. The right wing, using the fear of increased foreign immigration and high unemployment, sallied forth in local elections in Berlin and Hesse and won Parliament seats. The neo-Nazis, having failed with direct threats, violence, and terrorism, joined this political movement to gain a position legally to bring their ideology to fruition.

The West German government commissioned a study of radicals in Germany in 1980. By 1982, the results were published. Within the volume that developed the group profiles from both the right and the left, the conclusions set the tone for the government position on neo-Nazis.[61] The authors concluded that there was no crystallized terrorist group developed on the right or among the neo-Nazis. In addition, it was ascertained that violent actions that were promulgated by neo-Nazis were the work of individuals or splinter organizations and generally the involvement in such activities was of limited duration.[62] They did conclude, however, that the right-wing extremist organizations, both political and militant, backed the efforts of the most radical elements. This, of course, set the tone for the government's view of neo-Nazi groups and afforded these organizations a sense of security from the stricter laws that governed terrorists. The government study suggested, as well, that effective police actions were the dominant reason for the inability of the radical neo-Nazis to attain the level of terrorist unions.[63] Gordon Craig, a renowned historian of German history, showed caution in regards to the neo-Nazis in his social treatise of the Germans since World War II. In his book, *The Germans*, Craig worries about the tendency in the period from 1980 to 1982 for Germans to be susceptible to the arguments of Michael Kühnen and his neo-Nazis. He did allow, however, that the groups were still "minuscule" and not powerful enough to cause a real threat to society as a whole.[64]

A RAND Corporation study on trends in international terrorism viewed the neo-Nazis differently in 1984. By this time, the neo-Nazis were far more visible in their actions. The West German police became far more familiar with the international connections of the neo-Nazis and realized that a potential threat existed on the right. The study admitted to the increased police efforts to inhibit the threat of the neo-Nazis, but went on to say that "clandestine channels report a continued effort by neo-Nazis to plot violent actions."[65]

Neo-Nazi terrorist activities showed a decline in 1984 and

1985, but this coincided with the police actions against Hoffman's few remaining followers and the incarceration of both Manfred Roeder and Michael Kühnen. This appears to have been a watershed in neo-Nazi tactics. The viability and effectiveness of terrorism was necessarily reevaluated during this period. The results were a movement for unifying the neo-Nazis and other right-wing extremists into a political bloc.

John Ardagh, in his book, *Germany and the Germans*, which was published as recently as 1987, discounted the importance of neo-Nazism. He said "neo-Nazism is today a marginal phenomenon of little influence."[66] And yet, during this same time, the West German government's annual report on extremism, *Verfassungsschutzbericht*, clearly indicated that the numbers of right-wing activists were in excess of 25,000 and the numbers of neo-Nazis exceeded 1,400. These numbers, of course, represented a minute portion of the overall population, but did provide a kernel of hard-core radicalism upon which to build. In order to generate popular support, these extremists had only to find a rallying point. In 1988 and 1989, that point was found. The fears generated by unemployment and the seemingly endless immigration of foreigners into West Germany offered the perfect opportunity to obtain support for right-wing theses.

By February 1989, foreign fears of the neo-Nazis surfaced throughout Europe. The Bonn newspaper, *General Anzeiger*, stated that foreign news correspondents "foresaw increasing neo-Nazi strength" because of the local election results in West Germany.[67] The Paris newspaper, *Liberation*, was quoted in the Bonn paper as saying that the death of Franz Josef Strauss[68] of Bavaria left the potential for the right to develop strength in Germany.[69] Another Paris paper, *Les Echos*, questioned whether "time had dimmed the memories of the Germans," and "whether they (Germans) were ripe again for right-wing influence."[70] The *General Anzeiger* pointed out that the Israeli newspaper, *Haaretz*, underscored the rise of neo-Nazi influence in Germany.[71] Other foreign papers in Stockholm, Copenhagen, and Rome voiced the same reservations and fears about neo-Nazi influence that appeared to be gaining strength throughout German politics.

The West German government did not stand idly by during

this apparent move on the part of the right-wing extremists to bid for political power. Michael Kühnen's neo-Nazi group was banned just prior to the election in Hesse. Raids were conducted against his followers, which provided evidence of the wanton disregard that the neo-Nazis had for the anti-Nazi laws. The media was informed as to the amounts of Nazi propaganda found during these raids. This, however, did not deter Kühnen in his efforts to continue to develop a neo-Nazi following. Twice his groups were banned, and each time he changed the organization's name and continued in his quest to revive Hitler's NSDAP.

NOTES

1. Bernard Saper, "On Learning Terrorism," in *International Fascism: New Thoughts and New Approaches*, George L. Mosse, ed. (London: SAGE Publications, 1979), 13.

2. Christopher Dobson and Ronald Payne, *The Terrorists, Their Weapons, Leaders and Tactics* (New York: Facts on File, 1982), 3.

3. United States Army, *Army Regulation 190–56*, 1.

4. Jonah Alexander et al., "Terrorism: Future Threats and Responses," *Terrorism* 7, 4 (1985), 369.

5. Bonnie Cordes et al., eds., *Trends In International Terrorism, 1982 and 1983* (California: The Rand Corporation, 1984), 40.

6. Defense Intelligence Agency, *International Terrorism: A Compendium*, vol. 1, *Western Europe* (Washington, D.C.: U.S. Government Printing Office, 1988).

7. Irving Fetscher and Günter Rohrmoser, *Ideologen und Strategien* (Opladen: Westdeutscher Verlag GmbH, 1981), 263.

8. Paul Wilkinson, *The New Fascists*, (London: Grant McIntyre Ltd., 1981), 103.

9. Bundesminister des Innern, *Verfassungsschutzbericht, 1987* (Bonn: Graphische Betriebe GmbH, 1988), 122.

10. LEXIS/NEXIS, "Increased Neo-Nazi Violence Against Refugees in West Germany," *Reuter's North European Service* (5 September 1986).

11. Ibid.

12. Ibid.

13. J. F. Pilat, "Research Note: European Terrorism and the Euromissile," *Terrorism* 7, 1 (1984), 64.

14. Bundesminister des Innern, *Terroristen im Kampf gegen Recht und Menschen würde* (Bonn: BMI, 1985), 38.
15. Ibid.
16. Cordes et al., 40.
17. "Hess' Death Stirs West German New-Nazis," *The Associated Press*, 10 September 1987.
18. Ibid.
19. Wilkinson, 103–4.
20. Dobson and Payne, 171.
21. Bundesminister des Innern, *"Die Herausforderung unseres Demokratischen Rechtsstaates durch Rechtsextremisten"* (Paper delivered at a BMI conference on 11 November 1988), 3.
22. Ibid.
23. Ibid.
24. Ibid.
25. "Hess' Death Stirs West German New-Nazis."
26. Wilkinson, 111.
27. Bundesminister des Innern, *Verfassungsschutzbericht (1987)* 106.
28. H. J. Horchem, *Terrorism in West Germany, Conflict Studies* 186 (April 1986), 9.
29. Defense Intelligence Agency, *Terrorism Summary* 1 (February 1988), 1.
30. "Oktoberfest Toll Now 13: 99 Are Still Hospitalized," *The New York Times*, 8.
31. Horchem, 33.
32. Wilkinson, 127.
33. Cordes et al., 40.
34. Ibid.
35. Bruce Hoffman, *Right Wing Terrorism in Europe* (Santa Monica, CA: Rand Company, 1982), 6.
36. Horchem, 9.
37. Bundesminister des Innern, *Verfassungsschutzbericht (1987)*, 100.
38. Interview with Michael Kühnen, *Der Spiegel*, no. 13 (27 March 1989), 33–34.
39. "Rechtsextremism," *Der Spiegel*, no. 5 (30 January 1989), 48.
40. Ibid., 49.
41. *DPA* (Hamburg) 11 March 1989.
42. Bundesminister des Innern, *Verfassungsschutzbericht (1987)*, 101.
43. Ibid.

44. *Reuter's Daily Summary*, "Neo-Nazi Arsonist Jailed," Nov 9, 1987.

45. *Reuter's Daily Summary*, "Neo-Nazis On Trail in W. Germany," 20 Aug 87.

46. Bundesminister des Innern, *"Die Herausforderung unseres Demokratischen Rechtstaates durch Rechtsextremisten,"* 9.

47. Bundesminister des Innern, *Verfassungsschutzbericht (1987)*, 106.

48. Bundesminister des Innern, *"Herausforderung unseres Demokratischen Rechtstaates durch Rechtsextremisten,"* 8.

49. Ibid.

50. "Former Neo-Nazi Sentenced to 10 1/2 Years in Prison," *The Week in Germany*, 27 October 1986, 7.

51. Ibid., 6.

52. Ibid., 6.

53. Dobson and Payne, 147.

54. Wilkinson, 111.

55. Eva Kolinsky, "Terrorism in West Germany," in *The Threat of Terrorism*, ed. Juliet Lodge (Boulder, CO: Westview Press, 1988), 72.

56. Ibid.

57. Ibid., 73.

58. Kurt B. Tauber, *Beyond Eagle and Swastika* (Connecticut: Wesleyan University, 1967) 982.

59. Ibid.

60. Abraham Ashkenasi, *Modern German Nationalism* (Cambridge, MA: Schenkman Publishing, 1976), 218.

61. Wanda von Baeyer-Katte et al., *Gruppenprozesse* (Opladen: Westdeutscher Verlag GmbH, 1982) 443.

62. Ibid.

63. Ibid.

64. Gordon Craig, *The Germans* (New York: G. P. Putnam's Sons, 1982), 80.

65. Cordes et al., 40.

66. John Ardagh, *Germany and the Germans* (New York: Harper and Row, 1987), 389.

67. "Le Pen under the Germans," *General Anzeiger*, 1 February 1989, 2.

68. Franz Josef Strauss was one of the most powerful postwar politicians in West Germany. From the late 1940s until his death in 1988, Strauss was the key politician in the Bavarian Conservative Party (CSU). His methods were often read by other West Germans as directed toward the consolidation of Strauss's power in Bavaria, a

state in which the populace often considered themselves separate from the rest of Germany. Strauss's political antics included not only vying for power within the West German Parliament, but were often unilateral in making commitments for Bavaria that were generally considered federal responsibilities. In 1987, *Der Spiegel*, a German magazine, featured Franz Josef Strauss as the *"König"* (king) of Bavaria, a perception that many throughout West Germany had of the venerable Bavarian politician. Strauss was often considered by his peers as the one individual who was capable of controlling the conservative elements within Bavaria, and therefore was able to insure that the right-wing extremists remained quiescent.

69. "Le Pen under the Germans," *General Anzeiger*, 1 February 1989, 2.

70. Ibid.

71. Ibid.

6   International Connections

> No culture or political system is immune from the dangers of
> the fascist mentality, not even the people who have suffered
> most from the barbarity of fascism.
>
> Paul Wilkinson, *The New Fascists*
> (New York: Harper & Row, 1967), 145.

Although the term "neo-Nazi" was coined to suggest that right-
wing militants in West Germany were a later apparition of the
Nazis, many of the same ideologies and symbolisms of the Nazi
era permeated other democratic societies throughout the West.
Right-wing extremism evolved in many nations throughout the
1970s and 1980s. Although coming from different roots and
backgrounds, the commonality of using Nazi identifiers prevailed among a number of the organizations. Many of the
groups that were in the Americas and in Western Europe based
their concepts on NSDAP ideology and methods. Militarism,
racism, anti-Semitism, and nationalism seemed to be the most
common similarities. Many groups adopted uniforms and symbols that were very similar to those of Hitler's SA "brownshirt"
paramilitary organization as a method of identity. A good number also used a derivation of the swastika, or the SS symbol as
their official group identifier. It is probably safe to say that
most of these right-wing organizations began using the Nazi
symbols because of a need to associate with a strong historical

image predicated upon authority and ultraright-wing ideology. This, of course, was provided by the Nazi Party and the Third Reich.

What is interesting is that those disparate groups that developed throughout the Western world became associated during the 1970s and 1980s. "Neo-Nazi" became an appellation given to these diverse groups. Therefore, the small cadre of right-wing militants in West Germany were only one aspect of an international neo-Nazism that arose during the postwar era.

Neo-Nazism and neo-Fascism showed the ability to grow in a number of countries, albeit in only a minute fraction of the population. Great Britain, for example, still has a sizeable contingency of professed neo-Nazis, who refer to themselves as the "National Front." In addition, the emergence of the youth groups with extreme neo-Nazi tendencies, normally referred to as skinheads, not only began to plague Great Britain, but the ideology of these groups spread to the United States and Western Europe during the latter part of the 1980s.

French right-wing groups were also in evidence during the 1970s and 1980s. Although not as well publicized as the groups of Great Britain during these early years, these French groups, of which the best known is Le Pen's *Front National*, supported the international meetings that became important avenues for groups from the European, North American, and South American regions to exchange information and materials.[1]

The United States was the primary source of printed materials and propaganda during the 1980s for many of the European neo-Nazi groups, particularly those within West Germany. Dominating the right-wing extremist activities in the United States are such groups as the National Socialist German Worker's Organization, NSDAP-OA (Lincoln, Nebraska), "The Sword," "The Order," and "The White Aryan Resistance," only to name a few. The latter is one of the most recent groups responsible for the spread of neo-Nazism among U.S. youth through the skinhead subculture.[2] In addition, it is known that the Ku Klux Klan supported, and continues to support, right-wing extremism throughout the United States.

There were a number of instances over the past 15 years where groups of neo-Nazis have gathered, communicated, or trained with members of similar organizations from other countries. These connections provided propaganda materials and "common cause" support for all of the participants. A number of German neo-Nazi groups directly benefitted from these efforts.

As early as 1974, the League of St. George, a British neo-Nazi organization, attempted to develop relationships with groups located in continental Europe. An invitation was extended to the leading neo-Nazis throughout Europe, including such prominent organizations as the French FANE (*Fédération d'Action Nationale et Européene*), the United States NSDAP-AO, the U.S. Ku Klux Klan, the Belgium VMO (*Vlaamse Militanten Orde*), and the Dutch Nazi Northern League.[3] The invitation was designed to coordinate the activities and interests of these neo-Nazi groups and to promulgate publishing of materials that jointly supported neo-Nazi ideology. The key interests to the British neo-Nazis, who were attempting to coordinate the joint effort, revolved around the support of two West German neo-Nazis, Arnd Marx of the *Wehrsportgruppen Hoffman* and Manfred Roeder of the *Deutsche Aktionsgruppe*. Both of these men had been overtly active neo-Nazis and provided a sense of potential leadership to an international effort of cooperation.

The efforts of 1974 culminated in a large gathering of neo-Nazi groups in Brazil during the summer of 1978. Over 480 different groups met together in Brazil during this period, providing a loose alliance that exchanged information and intelligence, engaged in training, and traded arms.[4] This meeting was followed a year later with another large gathering of international neo-Nazis in Barcelona, Spain.

The summer of 1979 was also the period in which European fraternal relationships between neo-Nazis became more apparent. The *Vlaamse Militanten Orde* (Flemish Militant Order), which was the primary Belgium neo-Nazi organization, became the host for international neo-Nazi gatherings. This group, centered in the Antwerp region of Belgium, sponsored a training camp in the Ardennes Forest, adjacent to the Belgium-West German border. Seventy-five neo-Nazi representatives from Italy, France, Belgium, and West Germany attended this training in the spring of 1979.[5] The participants engaged in joint paramilitary maneuvers and were briefed on underground (guerrilla) warfare.[6]

A continuing effort for international cooperation was apparent throughout the early 1980s. Safehouses for neo-Nazi members being sought by their respective governments, propaganda materials, intelligence, arms, and training continued to be provided on a joint-effort basis among the different groups. In April 1987, the Belgium neo-Nazis again hosted a "European neo-Nazi Congress." The meetings were held near Antwerp, Belgium, and around 250 neo-Nazis participated. Representatives came from Belgium, France, Great Britain, the Netherlands, and West Germany. The joint resolution resulting from this conference declared that the representatives "supported a fight for a free and white Europe."[7] In addition, an action group was organized among the more militant European groups to fight under the name "Euroring" for the common goal of a "free and white Europe" as was identified by the entire congress.[8]

Not only were cooperative neo-Nazi organizational actions happening during the 1970s and 1980s, but joint efforts for life support activities were initiated. In 1979, the "Aid Association for National Political Prisoners and Their Relatives" was organized.[9] The organization was designed to coordinate neo-Nazi activities. The West German police considered this particular joint effort as an example of the coordination of international terrorist acts. This was the first major effort at developing an intercontinental support system. Belgian, Austrian, Swiss, and French neo–Nazis worked together to insure coordinated activities and provide adequate safehouses. Even the U.S. neo-Nazi and right-wing extremists provided support by insuring that adequate supplies of written neo-Nazi propaganda were available to the Europeans.

The West German police first became fully aware of the "Euro-Nazi" international network after arresting Manfred Roeder in 1980. Roeder had maintained a diary in which he kept an account of West German contacts with French, Italian, and Spanish neo-Nazis and neo-Fascists. Contained in this diary were highlights of U.S. neo-Nazi organizations' involvement with Europeans. Roeder showed proof of the active provisioning of Euro-Nazis with published materials by these U.S. organizations. In addition, the diary showed that fund-raising was very effective within the United States in support of Western European neo-Nazism.[10] In an article published in *Der Spiegel* in October 1980, it was alleged that specific ties existed between West German and U.S. groups, particularly the NSDAP-AO and the Ku Klux Klan.[11]

Not only did the neo-Nazis implement a program of international meetings and cooperative information systems over the last decade, but there were allegations that such activities as international right-wing programs, joint funding programs, and a worldwide arms network existed during this period.[12] These allegations were not substantiated, but European authorities believed that these types of cooperative ventures were occurring. Most of the evidence was obtained through interrogation of prisoners, which was enough to cause authorities to consider this cooperation as a potential threat from the Right.

However, coalescing of the right-wing militants, especially the neo-Nazis, was continually plagued with obstacles. The natural jealousies and rivalries that existed between the neo-Nazi groups insured that no one leader was able to bring the movement together for more than mere cooperation. In addition, the inherent nationalism that accompanied the separate European neo-Nazi organizations tended to preclude a truly "Euro-neo-Nazi" movement. Balancing out the triad of elements that inhibited an effective union of all neo-Nazis in Europe and America was the difference of language. Therefore, leadership rivalry, nationalism, and language were the key elements that insured a split among international neo-Nazis and provided the best sense of security to the governments.

In addition to the neo-Nazi cooperative actions, another type of internationalism developed during the late 1970s. Although the need for specific training in military guerrilla types of activities were of less importance to the more militant neo-Nazis, there were cases of international training that were conducted by Middle East contacts. The neo-Nazi movement proved to be far less dependent upon outside paramilitary training simply because of the inherent military status of the environment in which they developed.

There were, however, instances of neo-Nazi group involvement with the Middle East and North Africa. Although there was no direct evidence to support a connection between Nazis who had fled to these regions following World War II and the recent involvement of neo-Nazis, there were indicators. Following the war, a large number of Nazis, particularly SS, Wehrmacht officers, and Gestapo officials, left Germany and settled in North Africa and throughout the Arabian Middle East. In some cases, these men were included in their adopted country's governmental structure often within the security services. For example, Johann von Leers, the Nazi Student League ideological training chief and editor of Goebbel's propaganda sheet, *"Wille und Weg,"* escaped to Egypt and became the head of Egypt's anti-Israeli propaganda program.[13] He changed his name to Omar von Leers after assuming his new duties and accepting a new homeland. Other ex-Nazis were known to have emigrated to Iraq and Syria.

Palestinian and German right-wing extremists had had contacts as early as 1967. Following the six-day war with Israel, a quasi neo-Nazi group, referred to as the *Bund Heimattreuer Jugend,* founded a para-military organization, called the *Hilfskorps Arabien.* This small West German group was organized to help support the Palestinians against the Israelis. However, as was the case later in the 1970s and early 1980s, the relationship never developed and cooperation was extremely limited.

Another attempt was made to develop a working rapport with the Palestinians in 1969, when a number of ex-Nazis gathered in Madrid, Spain, to offer support for the PLO (Palestinian Liberation Organization) fighters. This support included an offer to provide instruction in guerrilla tactics and the publication of propaganda useful to the Palestinian cause. The more radical PLO faction, referred to as the "Popular Front for Liberation of Palestine" (PFLP), accepted the proposed concept. The PFLP leadership obtained a former Nazi military commander, who set up a guerrilla-type military training camp at

Basra, in southern Iraq.[14] The camp was the harbinger of training programs that developed over the next 20 years in Iraq, Syria, and Libya. These camps provided military and terrorist training to radical organizations from around the world, no matter what their individual ideology may have been.

Connections between the Arab regions and identified West German neo-Nazis began to appear in early 1970. An organization calling itself *Freikorps Adolf Hitler*, which was founded by Udo Albrecht, was identified as actively participating in the Palestinian Liberation Organization (PLO) "Black September" war against King Hussein's government in Jordan. Albrecht and 12 followers supported this extremely militant faction of the Palestinians and were reported to have fought alongside the PLO.

Udo Albrecht, himself, had a reputation for being a militant and having criminal instincts. From 1958 to the early 1980s, Albrecht was jailed 17 years and escaped no less than eight times.[15] In 1970 he was arrested in Germany and found to be carrying an identification card that connected him to the PLO Fatah organization, which was the largest PLO faction in the Middle East and the descendent of the "Black September" group out of Jordan. This arrest was the first direct proof to German police that there were connections between German radicals, in this case neo-Nazis, with the Middle East organizations that were known to use terrorism liberally. Once again, in 1975, Albrecht was implicated in an illegal activity utilizing Middle East connections while attempting to smuggle neo-Nazi literature from Germany to Lebanon. He and three companions were stopped at the border of Yugoslavia. Albrect escaped and the three companions were returned to Germany. Albrecht was captured in 1976 and imprisoned in Germany for two years.

The PLO contacts were then pursued by another neo-Nazi, Manfred Roeder. Following the suggestion of Albrecht, Roeder went to Lebanon to make contact with Yassir Arafat. However, he only spoke with Abu Jihad, Arafat's deputy. Jihad refused to cooperate with Roeder, thereby putting a damper on PLO and German neo-Nazi relations.

The international contacts with militant Palestinians were uncovered by West German officials in January of 1978. Members of both the *Hilfskorps Arabien*, and the newer neo-Nazi group *Freikorps Adolf Hitler*, were arrested for suspicion of smuggling arms from the Arab region into West Germany for the Palestinians that were living in Europe.[16]

Manfred Roeder's diary, which was obtained upon his arrest, provided information about not only European neo-Nazi connections, but also was explicit about his efforts to make connections in the Middle East. Roeder spent time attempting to obtain support for neo-Nazism in Europe, the Middle East, South America, and the United States during the late 1970s. As indicated earlier, his contacts with the PLO resulted in a total lack of cooperation. Roeder's goal was to obtain arms and monies for his West German neo-Nazi movement. However, since Roeder was unable to develop a good working relationship with the PLO or Iran, he then traveled to Itatataja, Brazil, and met with old Nazis in a German colony. Here he received a warm welcome and was offered the opportunity to speak and raise funds. After having tasted success in South America, Roeder proceeded on to the United States, where he met with Ku Klux Klan representatives and a member of a white supremist group called "Invisible Empire." These two groups then provided Roeder with moral support and some limited funds, which set the precedent for more support from neo-Nazis within the United States over the next decade.

Manfred Roeder did not give up on the potential for arms and money from the Middle East, particularly through the radical PLO elements. In 1980 he returned to Syria and Iraq and pursued a working relationship of mutual support and interest. Roeder was still unable to develop a rapport with any of the militant Arabs. This last effort spelled the end to efforts of obtaining direct logistical and financial support from the Middle East. This, however, did not preclude members of right-wing extremists, and particularly neo-Nazis, from participating in the growing numbers of terrorist training camps that sprang up around the Arab region.

Although Manfred Roeder was unable to develop a working relationship with the PLO, others of neo-Nazi persuasion were able to break down some of the barriers. Early in 1969, Jean Tereault, a Belgian, who was the secretary of the Belgian neo-

Nazi group called *La Natión Européene*, served as an advisor to the PLO Al Fatah organization. Another neo-Nazi from West Germany, Karl Heinz Hoffman, developed fairly close relations with the PLO. Hoffman's neo-Nazi group, *Wehrsportgruppen Hoffman*, was estimated by the West German government officials to have a membership of approximately 600 by the time the group was outlawed in early 1980. Attention was drawn to this particular group as they conducted war games with tanks and armored personnel carriers on Hoffman's property, a castle and grounds near Nuremberg.[17] Those who participated in these events wore uniforms, which were very similar to those worn by the SS during the 1930s and 1940s. This apparent disregard for the laws banning Nazi memorabilia and Nazi-oriented activities, and a move to terrorist types of actions, led to the eventual banning of the Hoffman group in January 1980. This, of course, did not stop Hoffman and a small group of his members from pursuing their goals outside of Germany.

Hoffman proceeded to Damascus, Syria, in July 1980, to develop links with PLO and East German intelligence agents.[18] Unlike Roeder, who was asking for help without much to offer in return, Hoffman working out of Lebanon developed a program that provided used trucks to the PLO in exchange for training.[19] Later in the summer of 1980, Hoffman and 15 members of his outlawed group went to a PLO Al Fatah training camp at Ben Hassan, south of Beirut. There they received training in paramilitary activities from PLO officers under the command of Abu Ayat, a central committee member of Al Fatah and the head of the PLO joint security forces.[20]

Returning to West Germany in late September, Hoffman and ten of the original 15 members who had gone to Lebanon soon used their newly acquired trade. During the Munich *Oktoberfest*, one member of the Hoffman group was killed during an attempt to place a bomb at the entrance of the festival. Then on 19 December 1980, Shlomo Levin, a 69-year-old Jewish publisher and his companion, Frieda Pöschke, were murdered at Levin's home with a submachine gun equipped with a silencer.[21] Investigators linked the returning Hoffman members to the killings.

Hoffman escaped back to Lebanon following these two incidents. He planned to set up a weapons factory in Lebanon that would provide adequate weapons to neo-Nazis in Europe. The West German police intercepted Hoffman and his girlfriend at the Frankfurt airport during an attempted secret trip into Germany in the late spring of 1981.

On 30 June 1986, Karl Heinz Hoffman was sentenced to nine years of prison in West Germany for weapons violations and for torturing people. He was acquitted of the murders of Levin and Pöschke because of the lack of evidence that could prove that he gave the orders for the victims' deaths. Hoffman, who was 48 years old at the time of his conviction, was jailed for possession of weapons and explosives, torturing members of his group, and for forging approximately two million dollars, which he used to finance his operations in Lebanon.[22]

The court proceedings, which took over 21 months, provided a glimpse into the sordid arrangements and procedures that Hoffman followed. The discipline and training were extremely difficult in the PLO training camp. Yet, in addition to the normal daily regimen, Hoffman forced his followers to meet higher standards. He used torture and beatings to force the group to exceed the minimums and to show their support of Hoffman's neo-Nazi program. Some were forced to smoke cigarettes made of dog hair and drink tea laced with nicotine.[23] One member was believed to have died from the abuse received at the camp.

The nine remaining Hoffman group members who were still alive were placed on trial in Nuremberg during November 1986. Charges ranged from grievous bodily harm to kidnapping and forgery.[24] These men ranged from 27 years of age to 48. All were past members of the outlawed *Wehrsportgruppen Hoffman*. They were convicted of the same types of crimes as Karl Hoffman was, and were imprisoned for similar periods of time. This effectively destroyed Hoffman's organization, turning the attention of the government officials to other neo-Nazi groups that were showing signs of increased activity, both politically and militantly, throughout West Germany.

After Hoffman's failure to develop a continuing program with the PLO and Roeder's total inability to secure support, the relationship between neo-Nazis and PLO radicals appeared to wane. Limited contacts surfaced in the later 1980s, but were still minimal. A Turkish Fascist organization's youth group, called the "Gray Wolves," developed some minor contacts with European neo-Nazis. This was arranged by an Azerbaijani called Mehmet Kengerle, who served with the Nazi SS during World War II.[25] This particular connection was not specifically defined, nor was it shown to be more than tentative.

France extradited an alleged neo-Nazi on charges of murder, armed bank robbery, and attempting to organize a right-wing terrorist group. Odfried Hepp, a 29-year-old West German national was arrested in Paris in April 1985 after having been implicated in a Lebanese guerrilla movement.[26] The murder charge that was the primary basis for extradition was related to a 1982 car bombing against a U.S. military member. French sources claimed that Hepp had specific links with Lebanese armed revolutionary factions, which were purported to have made gun and bomb attacks against U.S. and Israeli targets within France and Italy during the 1981–1984 period.[27]

The European neo-Nazi efforts, particularly those groups in West Germany, to develop international cooperation showed mixed results. The European neo-Nazis continued to develop cooperative programs throughout the late 1970s and well into the 1980s. The annual meetings hosted by the Belgian VMO neo-Nazi organization drew together more international representatives each year. Joint efforts between countries to preclude these joint events proved to be ineffective for stopping their continuation. The neo-Nazis were able to maintain contacts throughout Europe and the United States and to obtain propaganda materials that were used to increase interest among the unemployed youth.

The inability of these divergent organizations to coalesce into an international neo-Nazi movement was primarily due to the natural rivalries that existed in their organizational structure. Militarily oriented, and extremely nationalist, these neo-Nazi groups have the seeds of factionalism embedded in their ideology.

NOTES

1. Bundesminister des Innern, *Verfassungsschutzbericht, 1987* (Bonn: Graphische Betriebe GmbH, 1988), 122.

2. "200 Protest Neo-Nazi Gathering," *The Stars And Stripes*, 12 December 1988, p. 8. The presence of these radical youth groups caused concern in the western United States. On 9 December 1988, a group of skinheads gathered in Freeland, Washington, to commemorate the death of Robert Mathews, founder of the violent neo-Nazi group called "The Order." Mathews died in December 1984 during a shoot-out with FBI agents. A number of Mathews's followers were convicted shortly after his death for robbing four million dollars and for the murder of Alan Berg, a Jewish talk-show host in Denver, Colorado. The result of the commemorative gathering was a large anti-Nazi gathering designed to counteract the skinhead program.

3. Paul Wilkinson, *The New Fascists* (London: Grant McIntyre Ltd., 1981), 88.

4. Bruce Hoffman, *Right-Wing Terrorism in Europe* (Santa Monica, CA.: Rand Company, 1982), 20.

5. Ibid., 22.

6. Ibid.

7. Bundesminister des Innern, *Verfassungsschutzbericht (1987)*, 122.

8. Ibid.

9. Eva Kolinsky, "Terrorism In West Germany," in *The Threat Of Terrorism*, ed. Juliet Lodge (Boulder, CO: Westview Press, 1988), 80.

10. Wilkinson, 125.

11. "Long Live Fascism," *Der Spiegel* (Hamburg), 6 October 1980, 46.

12. Hoffman, 22.

13. Kurt Tauber, *Beyond Eagle and Swastika* (Connecticut: Wesleyan University, 1967), 174–76.

14. Wilkinson, 125.

15. H. J. Horchem, "European Terrorism: A German Perspective," in *Terrorism*, vol. 6, no. 1 (New York: Crane, Russak, Francis & Taylor Group, 1982), 36.

16. Ibid., 126.

17. "West Germany Jails Neo-Nazi for Nine Years," *The Los Angeles Times*, June 30, 1986, 1.

18. Hoffman, 21.

19. Ibid.

20. Horchem, 37.

21. "West Germany Jails Neo-Nazi for Nine Years," 1.

22. Ibid.

23. "Nine Neo-Nazis Go on Trial in West Germany," *Reuter's Daily Summary*, 13 November 1986.

24. Ibid.

25. Wilkinson, 128.

26. "France Extradites Alleged Neo-Nazi to West Germany," *Reuter's Daily Summary*, 3 February 1987.

27. Ibid.

7   The Nazi Legacy and
       the Future

Speaking of the Nazis, do you think these agitators will ever
get anywhere?

Robert Murphy, U.S. Foreign Service as quoted in
Charles Bracelen Flood, *Hitler: The Path to Power*
(Boston: Houghton Mifflin Co., 1989), 237.

The term "neo-Nazi" has evolved into a generic word in Germany over the past four decades. Whenever a right-wing
extremist group, whether political or militant, supports rightist
interests, they are often labeled as neo-Nazis. This, however,
tends to obscure the real neo-Nazi movement that is associated
with the most militant of the ultra-right. What is certain is
that the militant right-wing tends to hover on the edges of less
extreme right-wing groups and often participate in those organization's political and social programs. This leads many in
Germany to classify the total rightist group as Nazi oriented.
It is often difficult to separate the radicals from the moderates
and therefore the government is at a disadvantage in determining the potential threat that may result from these
organizations.

A good example of this problem is shown with the German
Republican Party (REP). Many of the critics have classified
this political entity as neo-Nazi. This was predicated on the

leadership, which has Nazi roots, and the interpretation of the political goals placed before the electorate in 1989 and 1990. However, in order for the Republican Party to remain a viable political entity within Germany, they must eliminate the appearance of being neo-Nazi and provide a platform that insures a means of meeting the needs of the population.

Early REP successes in 1989 were followed by major losses in the 1990 elections. The electoral support for right-wing candidates dissipated quickly in the new elections, showing that the voters probably used the right wing to make a point with the existing conservative political parties. These parties, the CDU and CSU, were out of touch with a portion of the electorate. The voters who supported the Republicans perceived that the issues dealing with ecology, immigration, and the economy were less important to the governing party than they should have been.

A primary reason for the short-lived strength of the right-wing political fortunes was the lack of definitive long-range goals and objectives. The platform of the Republicans was predicated on issues rather than ideology. By attacking the existing party and governmental methods of dealing with issues that directly influenced the population, the Republican candidates offered the opportunity for a short-term emotional response to the problems facing modern Germany. There was little offered that would indicate that the right-wing planned to address the problems and find solutions. Instead, the party placed emphasis on the mobilization of feelings among the population against individual shortcomings. They accomplished this by exploiting fears associated with the changes in the Germany society and modernization. Therefore, the voters responded with votes against present conditions and not against the existing parties. A foundation of right-wing voters was not established. This left the rightist parties, particularly the Republicans, with little popular support. The result of these shortcomings was a Republican Party which experienced a fracturing of its leadership during the summer of 1990. The more radical members, primarily from Bavaria, broke away from the traditional leader, Schönhuber, thereby greatly weakening the party. The future of the Republican Party is tenuous, but not necessarily terminated.

The right wing does have a potential following in East Germany. Unification of Germany afforded the Republican Party a source of support. Not only does the right-wing political opportunity exist, but the militant neo-Nazis found a possible area for recruiting. Michael Kühnen went to the German Democratic Republic in January 1990 to generate support for his right-wing neo-Nazi programs. He was successful in recruiting approximately 100 members for his new East German "protest party," referred to as the German Alternative (DA).[1]

The right-wing extremists and militants share some of the same opportunities in the eastern part of Germany. The unemployment rate in East Germany rose from 130,000 in June 1990 to 273,000 in July of the same year.[2] This places a tremendous strain on the CDU and SPD, which are presently the dominant parties in German politics, in their efforts to consolidate and effectively govern a country which has been so diverse in lifestyle and government for over 45 years. East Germans were under Communist rule for such a length of time that a whole generation is unaware of democratic principles. Moving from a socialist system to one of capitalism has forced businesses that traditionally were dependent on the State to insure survival to become competitive. This means improved technology and a new work ethic, both of which are proving difficult to obtain. The result was rising unemployment and an increasing fear of the future among the working class and younger population.

From March through the early summer months of 1990, the right wing made a visible impact on many of the East German youth. Rallies became a weekly affair in many parts of East Germany. Groups of disenchanted East Germans marched and shouted old Nazi slogans and literally used the arm salute that was so familiar from the NSDAP membership.[3] In addition, there were increased incidents of attacks against foreign workers and extensive use of graffiti that was aimed against the Jewish population. These activities were directly attributed to young factory workers, who were labeled as skinheads.[4]

The World Soccer Cup championships during July 1990 punctuated the intensity of the right-wing militancy movement in East Germany. East Berlin began the celebration of the German win in the championships with cheer and excitement. The joy of winning soon turned to bitterness as violence spread throughout northern Germany. Youth, identified as neo-Nazi skinheads, brawled with police in East Berlin, Hamburg, and Bielefeld.[5] Foreigners were singled out for attacks, four people were killed, hundreds were injured—of which 60 were police— and over 120 were arrested.[6]

Are the neo-Nazis a viable future threat? Is history being repeated in the latter part of the twentieth century? Robert Murphy, a U.S. diplomat assigned to the Bavarian Consulate in the early 1920s, queried a German national employee about the future of the Nazis. That employee, Paul Drey, responded, "Of course not! The German people are too intelligent to be taken in by such scamps."[7] Interestingly, once again in the twentieth century, the specter of right-wing radicalism, with strong antiforeign prejudices and a burning desire for nationalist identity, has raised its head. History provided the reason for extinguishing the Nazi ideology, and yet, as more time lapsed from the end of the Third Reich, it also afforded the ultra-right a chance to identify with an organization that appealed to their militant approach.

It appears, from the available evidence, that postwar German neo-Nazi roots are linked to Hitler's Third Reich. This is evidenced by the numbers of ex-Nazis who continued to implant Nazi ideology into the political system and influence West German youth during the 40 years following the war. Although neo-Nazism was not directly apparent until the late 1970s, the right-wing extremism that bordered on Nazism was entrenched in a minority of the West German population. This became clear immediately following the establishment of the Federal Republic of Germany. Political parties, which were epitomized by the Socialist Reich Party (SRP), and later by the Nationalist Germany Party (NPD), were dominated by ex-Nazis and the ideologies were reminiscent of that of the NSDAP. The similarities continued to surface in right-wing extremist organizations during the four decades following the war's end.

The fears of the West German government that Nazism would be retained in their society became fact. The war generation carried many of the Nazi ideas into the postwar period. War veterans that became advocates of the Third Reich were able to provide a basis for the continuation of Nazi ideology and symbolism. Many young Germans, having a void in their historical perspectives due to the prohibition of Nazi history in schools and in society, became members of a group that filled that void. The *Main Post*, a Würzburg newspaper, acknowledged this national shortcoming in November 1988 when an article stated: "as long as we still encounter tremendous gaps in the historic thinking of many of the younger citizens about the insanity of the National Socialist regime there is a need to use every occasion to deepen at least our basic awareness."[8]

These youth were often looking for a source of close companionship and support in their quest to find a position in the evermore complex industrial society. The neo-Nazis provided an authoritative, yet close-knit organization that played on the fears and the needs of these young people. Once again the past returned to haunt those who saw the results of Hitler's Nazi program. The neo-Nazis became far more open and vocal in the 1980s. Their extremism harkens back to the early 1920s, when Hitler and his followers began to develop an organization that brought Europe into a world war. The world conditions are not the same as those in the 1920s and 1930s, therefore the chances of the neo-Nazi movement becoming more than a fringe element are extremely limited. However, the militancy of this group provides adequate resources for potential terrorist options.

If the right-wing militants are unable to incorporate their interests into the existing political system, the option of terror is still available. The militants on the radical fringes of German conservatism may become frustrated with the slow process of politics, or the less radical positions taken by the extremist faction, making them a minority to be recognized and dealt with in the future. This frustration, tied to the links with Middle East terrorist groups, can make these groups volatile. There were indications during 1990 that there were increased contacts between right-wing militants and the Iranian-backed terrorist organization, *Hezbollah*.[9] The Central Intelligence Agency became convinced that large quantities of arms were smuggled into southern Europe from the Middle East.[10] Over 500 pounds of C-4 explosive was discovered by the Spanish police in Valencia, Spain, in November 1989. The explosives were found hidden in 25,000 jars of jam being shipped to Germany from the Lebanese port of Sidon.[11]

With the unification of Germany, the German nationalist radicals may find an excuse to attack Allied troops still located within Germany in order to hasten departure of the perceived occupiers. This raises the fear of attacks by newly armed right-wing militant groups on both U.S. military and diplomatic targets in Germany.

In summary, the increased interest among the West Germans over the growing radicalism and membership in neo-Nazi organizations provided the impetus for this study on postwar German right-wing extremism.[12] An important aspect of the growth of this extremist movement is the possible connection that existed between the "old line" Nazis of Hitler's era and those who became active neo-Nazis in the 1980s.

Within the discussion of the development of the present neo-Nazi groups, it is important to consider the right-wing organizations from which many of the members were recruited or obtained. A number of political parties and youth groups, which represented various right-wing interests, existed in West German society after 1945. These organizations varied from the moderate right to the more radical militant right wing. On a continuum, the CDU/CSU generally represented the conservative moderates and the NPD and Republicans the more extreme. Far to the right, representing the militant elements, were the neo-Nazis. It is important to consider these organizations, and their roles, when discussing the rise of right-wing extremism. What is clear is that many of the most radical members of the neo-Nazi groups were originally associated with legally constituted organizations that were traditionally classified as having rightist interests. Often, these more radical elements were the ones who became the hard-core ideologists in the underground militant groups and, therefore, were most likely to participate in terrorist activities.

One important aspect of the postwar neo-Nazi movement was the internationalism that developed. Almost annually, from 1978 to 1988, representatives of neo-Nazi groups from Europe, the United States, and South America, met and exchanged information, propaganda, and ideas. A continuing problem of leadership and the individuality of the many diverse groups tended to diminish the possibilities of a truly united international neo-Nazi movement.

Although only a small fraction of the German population condones the neo-Nazi's actions, and only a minute number of militants are active, the use of terror was introduced in early 1980 and was used selectively for the next seven years. Although these acts of violence dwindled drastically in the latter 1980s, the opportunity remained.

Terrorist acts tend to draw attention to minority positions, as was evidenced by the publicity that the leftist Red Army Faction obtained. Facing laws that deny the rights of Nazis to exist in Germany, and unable to provide viable input into the political system, many frustrated neo-Nazi elements considered the use of terrorism. This was evidenced by the gathering of arms and munitions, as well as open acts of violence. As occurred with the left-wing Baader-Meinhof group in the late 1960s, the right-wing extremists of the early 1980s showed that terrorist actions could, and would, be used. Terrorism is being used throughout the world by minority groups that are excluded from the political processes. This method of political statement is extremely difficult for democracies to overcome, due primarily to human rights considerations. Neo-Nazis showed a willingness to use terrorism in the early 1980s and presumably could use it again. The evolution of the militant right wing is important to Germany and to the nations in which neo-Nazism has developed and grown. The possibility of having right-wing terror reaching the same sophistication that many of the left-wing groups have attained is frightening. At present, the neo-Nazis do not present a major threat, but they do have a history, albeit short, of using terrorism, which could propel them into a far more visible arena.

NOTES

1. *"Schon Gehuscht," Der Spiegel*, no. 3, 15 January 1990, 76.
2. United States Department of State, Bureau of Public Affairs, *Bulletin 23*, 24 August 1990, 3.
3. David Bender, "Violence by Skinheads Startling East Germans," *The New York Times*, 21 August 1990, 1 A2.
4. Ibid.
5. "Violence, Death Mar German's Victory Rites," *Dayton Daily News* (Dayton, Ohio), 10 July 1990, 4A.
6. Ibid.
7. Charles Bracelen Flood, *Hitler: The Path To Power* (Boston: Houghton Mifflin Company, 1989), 237.
8. *Main Post* (Würzburg), 8 November 1988, as quoted in the weekly compilation, *The Week In Germany* (New York, 10 November 1988), 3.
9. "Hezbollah, Extremists Linked," *Washington Times*, 6 February 1990, 8.
10. Ibid.
11. Ibid.
12. As recently as 9 February 1989, the Federal Republic of Germany outlawed the major neo-Nazi organization, *Nationale Sammlung*. This group had fielded candidates for Frankfurt's elections in March 1989. Raids on this organization yielded numerous weapons and large numbers of Nazi posters and banners. The ban forbids the organization from group activities and public use of their name. In an article entitled, "W. Germany Raids, Bans Neo-Nazi Unit," *Dayton (Ohio) Daily News*, 10 February 1989, sec. C, p. 12, the comment was made that this event "coincides with a growing concern in West Germany of a possible resurgence of ultra-rightist tendencies."

Selected Bibliography

BOOKS

Alexander, Jonah, David Carlton, and Paul Wilkinson, *Terrorism: Theory and Practice.* Colorado: Westview Press, 1979.

Allen, William S. *The Nazi Seizure of Power.* Chicago: Quandrangle Books, 1965. A study of the development of the NSDAP in a small, central German town. This book looks at the individuals involved in the Nazi Party and the reactions of the local populace during the growth of Nazi power.

Ardagh, John. *Germany and the Germans.* New York: Harper and Row, 1987. The author provides an interesting analysis of the development of modern German social values. This was done by using personal contacts and interviews.

Ashkenasi Abraham. *Modern German Nationalism.* Cambridge, Massachusetts: Schenkman Publishing Company, 1976.

Baeyer-Katte, Wanda von, Dieter Claessens, Hubert Feger, Friedhelm Neidhardt. *Gruppenprozesse.* Opladen: Westdeutscher Verlag GmbH, 1982. A study prepared for the Ministry of Interior, in response to a need for evaluating the terrorist threat in West Germany. This analysis covered the environments and processes that were used to obtain members for extremist groups within West Germany.

Becker, Jillian. *Hitler's Children: The Story of the Baader-Meinhof Terrorist Gang.* Philadelphia: J. B. Lippincott, 1977.

Brozart, Martin. *Hitler and the Collapse of Weimar Germany.* New York: Berg Publishers, 1987.

Carlton, David, and Carlo Schaerf, eds. *Contemporary Terror*. London: Macmillian, 1981.

Chafe, William H. *The Unfinished Journey*. New York: Oxford University Press, 1986. General United States history. Short, but concise, discussion of Morgenthau's plans for Germany. Relationship of Roosevelt to the plan and the decision by Truman to implement the Marshall Plan.

Cordes, Bonnie, Bruce Hoffman, Brian Jenkins, Konrad Kellen, Sue Moran, William Sater. *Trends in International Terrorism, 1982 and 1983*. California: The Rand Corporation, 1984.

Craig, Gordon A. *Europe Since 1815*. New York: Holt, Rinehart and Winston, 1971. A general history text with a strong German section.

————. *Germany, 1866–1945*. New York: Oxford University Press, 1978.

————. *The Germans*. New York: G. P. Putnam's Sons, 1982. An excellent discussion of present-day Germany and the people. Some of this study refers to the right wing, particularly the neo-Nazis, within modern West Germany.

Dobson, Christopher, and Ronald Payne. *The Terrorists, Their Weapons, Leaders, and Tactics*. New York: Facts On File, 1982.

Eisenberg, Dennis. *The Re-emergence of Fascism*. New York: A. S. Barnes and Company, 1967.

Elliot, John D., and Leslie K. Gibson, eds. *Contemporary Terrorism*. Maryland: International Association of Chiefs of Police, 1978.

Emmet, Christopher, and Norbert Muhlen. *The Vanishing Swastika*. Chicago: Henry Regenery Company, 1961.

Fetscher, Iring and Günter Rohrmoser. *Ideologen und Strategien*. Opladen: Westdeutscher Verlag GmbH, 1981.

Flood, Charles Bracelen. *Hitler: The Path To Power*. Boston: Houghton Mifflin Company, 1989. A newly published treatise on the early Nazi organization and Hitler's role.

Forman, James D. *Nazism*. New York: Dell Publishing Company, 1978.

Glicksman, William. "Violence and Terror: The Nazi-German Conception of Killing and Murder." *International Terrorism in the Contemporary World*. Westport, CT: Greenwood Press, 1978, 432.

Gregor, James A. *Italian Fascism and Developmental Dictatorship*. New Jersey: Princeton University Press, 1979.

Grill, Johnpeter Horst. *The Nazi Movement in Baden, 1920–1945*. Chapel Hill, North Carolina: University of North Carolina

Press, 1983. An expanded dissertation on the development of the Nazi Party in Baden (Southern Germany) using primary records of the State of Baden and the local NSDAP.

Herzstein, Robert E. *Waldheim: The Missing Years*. New York: Arbor House/William Morrow, 1988. Provides an overview of the war years and Kurt Waldheim's involvement with the Nazi war crimes in Yugoslavia and Greece. Provides information on the denazification program and the rise of National Socialism in Austria.

Hitler, Adolf. *Mein Kampf*. Unabridged edition, translated, John Chamberlain et al., eds. Boston: Houghton Mifflin Company, 1939.

Hoffman, Bruce. *Right-wing Terrorism in Europe*. Santa Monica, CA: Rand Company, 1982. A short report on right-wing terrorism prepared for the U.S. Air Force. Provides a brief discussion of French, West German, and Italian neo-Nazi groups and the increase in activities in early 1980s.

Horchem, H. J. *West Germany's Red Army Anarchists*. London: Conflict Studies, no. 46, 1974.

Irving, David. *Göring: A Biography*. New York: William Morrow and Company, 1989. A biography of Hermann Göring. The book delves into Göring's relationships with Hitler and other high-level Nazis. Discusses Göring's weakness of finery and his turbulent private life.

Jäger, Herbert, Gerhard Schmidtchen, Lieselotte Süllwold. *Lebenslaufanalyses*. Opladen: Westdeutscher Verlag GmbH, 1981.

Janke, Peter. *Guerrilla and Terrorist Organizations: A World Directory and Bibliography*. New York: Macmillan Publishing Company, 1983. An excellent resource of specific terrorist organizations and their vital statistics.

Knütter, Hans-Helmuth. *Ideologien des Rechtsradikalismus im Nachkriegsdeutschland*. Bonn: Ludwig Röhrscheid Verlag, 1961.

Kolinsky, Eva. "Terrorism In West Germany." In *The Threat of Terrorism*, ed. Juliet Lodge, 57–88. Boulder, CO: Westview Press, 1988.

Laqueur, Walter. *The Age of Terrorism*. Boston: Little, Brown and Company, 1987.

———. *Germany Today*. Boston: Little, Brown and Company, 1985.

———. *The Terrorism Reader: A Historical Anthology*. Philadelphia: Temple University Press, 1978.

Linklater, Magnus, Isabel Hilton, and Neal Ascherson. *The Nazi Legacy*. New York: Holt, Rinehart and Winston, 1984. Biography of Klaus Barbie, head of the Nazi SD in Lyon, France.

Livingston, Marius H., ed. *International Terrorism In The Contemporary World.* Connecticut: Greenwood Press, 1978.

Ludecke, Kurt W. G. *I Knew Hitler: A Story of a Nazi Who Escaped the Blood Purge.* London: National Book Association, 1938.

Lyttelton, Adrian, ed. *Italian Fascism: From Pareto to Gentile.* New York: Harper and Row, 1973.

Matz, Ulrich, and Gerhard Schmidtchen. *Gewalt and Legitimität.* Opladen: Westdeutscher Verlag GmbH, 1983.

Mosse, George L., ed. *International Fascism: New Thoughts and New Approaches.* London: SAGE Publications, 1979.

————. *Masses and Man: Nationalist and Fascist Perceptions of Reality.* New York: H. Fertig, 1980. Series of essays written by Mosse over the past years. These essays reflect on the development of nationalism and the use of this term to provide a sense of control by different peoples.

————. *Nazism.* New Jersey: Transaction, 1978.

O'Donnell, James P. *The Bunker.* Boston: Houghton Mifflin Company, 1978. A short book about Hitler's final days in the bunker in Berlin. The author used interviews following the war to reconstruct the events.

von Oppen, Beate Ruhm. *Documents of Germany Under Occupation, 1945–1954.* London: Oxford University Press, 1955. Translated postwar documents dealing with the Allied occupation of Germany.

Payne, Stanley G. *Fascism: Comparison and Definition.* Madison, WI: University of Wisconsin Press, 1980. Systematic approach to define characteristics and make distinctions on a broad comparative basis of different Fascist movements in Europe (includes Nazism).

Sack, Fritz, and Heinz Steinert. *Protest und Reaktion.* Opladen: Westdeutscher Verlag GmbH, 1984. Deals with the handling of terrorism within West German law.

Schlagheck, Donna. *International Terrorism: An Introduction to the Concepts and Actors.* Massachusetts: Lexington Books, 1988.

Schuech, Erwin K. *"Politischer Extremismus in der Bundesrepublik."* *Die Zweite Republik, 25 Jahre Bundesrepublik Deutschland-eine Bilanz,* ed. by Richard Löwenthal and Hans-Peter Schwartz. Stuttgart: Seewald Verlag, 1974.

Schwind, H. D. *Ursachen des Terrorismus der Bundesrepublik.* Berlin: Walter de Gruyter, 1978. An excellent breakdown of the demographics of peoples involved in both right- and left-wing extremism in West Germany.

Segev, Tom. *Soldiers of Evil*. New York: McGraw-Hill, 1987. An excellent look at the commandants of Nazi concentration camps, which includes a good accounting for the reasons for many to join the Nazi SS.

Shirer, William. *The Rise and Fall of the Third Reich*. New York: Simon and Schuster, 1960.

Stachura, Peter D. *The German Youth Movement, 1900–1945*. New York: St. Martin's Press, 1981.

Starr, Joseph R. *Denazification, Occupation and Control of Germany, March–July, 1945*. Salisbury, NC: Documentary Publications, 1977. Monograph written in 1950 for the U.S. Army. Classified until 1975.

Sterling, Claire. *The Terror Network*. New York: Holt, Rinehart and Winston, 1981.

Tabbora, Lina. *Survivre dans Beyrouth*. Paris: Olivier Orban, 1977.

Tauber, Kurt B. *Beyond Eagle and Swastika*. Connecticut: Wesleyan University, 1967.

Thackrah, John Richard. *Encyclopedia of Terrorism and Political Violence*. New York: Routledge and Kegan Paul, 1987.

Weiss, John. *The Fascist Tradition*. New York: Harper and Row, 1967.

Wilkinson, Paul. *The New Fascists*. London: Grant McIntyre Ltd., 1981.

———. *Political Terrorism*. New York: Halstead Press, 1976.

———. *Terrorism and the Liberal State*. New York: New York University Press, 1985.

Ziemke, Earl F. *The U.S. Army in the Occupation of Germany, 1944–1946*. Washington, DC: Center of Military History, U.S. Army, 1975.

ARTICLES, STUDIES, AND PAPERS

Alexander, Jonah, Phil Baum, and Raphael Danziger, eds. "Terrorism: Future Threats and Responses." *Terrorism* 7, 4 (1985).

Andresen, Karen. "Der Hässliche Deutsche." *Stern Magazine* 6, 2 (February 1989).

Berger, Manfred, Wolfgang G. Gibowski, and Dieter Roth. "Movement On The Right Edge: The Small Radical Parties the Big Winners, Analysis of the Baden-Wuerttemberg Election Results." *Die Zeit*, 25 March 1988, 5.

Böhme, Erich. "*Der Rock rutscht hoch.*" *Der Spiegel*, 6 February 1989, 6.

Bundesminister des Innern. "*Die Herausforderung unseres Demok-*

ratischen Rechtstaates durch Rechtsextremisten." Paper presented in conference. 11 November 1988. A paper presented in a seminar by a member of the Interior Minister's antiterrorism office. Addresses the growth of right-wing extremism in West Germany.

———. *Verfassungsschutzbericht, 1984.* Bonn: Graphische Betriebe GmbH, 1985.

———. *Verfassungsschutzbericht, 1987.* Bonn: Graphische Betriebe GmbH, 1988.

Control Council, Allied Occupation Forces, United States Zone, West Germany. *Official Gazette,* no. 1, 29 October 1945.

———. *Official Gazette,* no. 5, 31 March 1946.

Dayton Daily News (Ohio). "West Germany Raids, Bans Neo-Nazi Unit," 10 February 1989, 12c.

Defense Intelligence Agency. *International Terrorism: A Compendium,* vol. I, Western Europe. Washington, DC: U.S. Government, February 1988.

Der Spiegel, 5. "*Rechtsextremismus.*" 30 January 1989, 12.

———, 7. "*Sympathisanten hinter den Gardinen.*" 13 February 1989, 54–64.

———, 6. "*Unser Endziel ist der Bundestag.*" 6 February 1989.

Die Welt. "*Die Republikaner sind eine rechte Protestpartei, die von Freiräumen lebt.*" 2 February 1989, 5.

———. "*Kohl: Die Union muss Republikaner bekämpfen.*" 15 February 1989, 10.

———. "Republican Party Chairman Views Election." 31 January 1989, 4.

Domando, Mario. "The German Youth Movement." Ph.D diss., Columbia University, 1960.

The Economist. "The Mark of the Far Right." 4 October 1980, 48.

General Anzeiger. "Bündnis der Vernunft." 31 January 1989, 2.

———. "*CDU/FDP Koalition verliert Mehrheit in Berlin.*" 30 January 1989, 1.

———. "*Der rechte Rand rückt auf.*" 30 January 1989, 1.

———. "*Die Berliner wollten ihre alte Regierung loswerden.*" 31 January 1989, 13.

———. "*Heftiger Streit in der Union um künftigen Kurs.*" 31 January 1989, 1.

———. "Le Pen under the Germans." 1 February 1989, 1.

———. "*Nach dem Wahlerfolg der Grössenwahn.*" 2 February 1989, 3.

———. "*Neofaschismus nicht Verharmlosen.*" 21 December 1988, 1.

————. "Neo-Nazi Kühnen Organizes a New Organization." 11 February 1989, 1.

————. *"Niemand redet mit den Republikanern."* 31 January 1989, 3.

————. *"NPD will gegen Verbot ihres Parteitages vorgehen."* 9 February 1989, 2.

————. *"Schönhuber sucht Gegenkandidaten zu Weizäcker."* 2 February 1989, 1.

————. *"SPD fordert Verfassungsschutz zur Beobachtung der Republikaner auf."* 3 February 1989, 2.

————. *"Wir werden Europa zum Beben bringen."* 9 February 1989, 3.

————. "Zimmerman Speaks About the Blow Against the Neo-Nazis." 10 February 1989.

Gläser, Hermann. *"Die Diskussion über den Terrorismus: Ein Dossier."* Aus Politik und Zeitsgeschichte Beilage zur Wochenzeitung das Parlament, 24 June 1978.

Günter, Harald. *"Schlee: Republikaner keine extremistische Partei."* *Die Welt,* 15 February 1989, 4.

Held, Joseph. "Embattled Youth: The Independent German Movements in the 20th Century." Ph.D. diss., Rutgers University, 1968.

Horchem, Hans Josef. "European Terrorism: A German Perspective," *Terrorism* 6, 1 (1982).

————. "Terrorism in West Germany," *Conflict Studies* 186 (April 1986). A paper presented at the International Academic Conference on Research Of Terrorism, Aberdeen University, April 1986.

Johnson, Chalmers. "Perspectives on Terrorism." *The Terrorism Reader,* Walter Laqueur, ed. Philadelphia: Temple University Press, 1978. 267–85. Review of a State Department sponsored conference held on March 25–26, 1976. Around 200 American and foreign specialists discussed problems dealing with terrorism.

Los Angeles Times. "West Germany Jails Neo-Nazi For Nine Years," 30 June 1986.

National Foreign Assessment Center. "Patterns of International Terrorism: 1980." Director of Public Affairs, CIA, 1981.

New York Times. "Links Between PLO and Neo-Nazis Seen." 1 October 1980, 2.

————. "Neo-Nazi Group Suspected in Blast That Killed 12 at Munich Festival." 29 September 1980, 4.

————. "Oktoberfest Toll Now 13: 99 Are Still Hospitalized." 2 October 1980, 8.

———. "Two Tied to German Neo-Nazis Are Suspects in Jew's Murder." 20 August 1981, 20.

Pilat, J. K. "Research Note: European Terrorism and the Euromissile." *Terrorism* 7, 1 (1984).

Reuter Library Service. "Jewish Leader Warns of Neo-Nazi Resurgence in West Germany," 22 March 1988.

Risks International, Inc. *Executive Risk Assessment* 1, 7 (May 1979), 3.

Saper, Bernard, "On Learning Terrorism." *Terrorism* 11, 1 (1988).

Schmemann, Serge. "Far-Right Victory Stirs High Anxiety in Berlin." *New York Times*, 31 January 1989.

Shipley, Peter. "Patterns of Protest in Western Europe." *Conflict Studies* 189 (1988).

Statistische Bundesamt. *Statistische Jahrbuch für die Bundesrepublik Deutschland, 1969, 1974, 1980.* Wiesbaden, Federal Republic of Germany.

Stern Magazine, 7. "Sauber, fleissig, ehrlich." 9 February 1989, 8–20.

Szabo, Stephen F. "Political Shifts in West Germany." *Current History* (November 1988), 361–64.

Vinocur, John. "Foreign Workers in West Germany Live Under the Shadow of Prejudice." *New York Times*, 22 February 1982.

Wittke, Thomas. "Alarm In Berlin." *General Anzeiger (Bonn)*, 30 January 1989, 2.

Zink, Harold. "The American Denazification Program in Germany." *Journal of Central European Affairs* 6 (October 1946).

Index

ABOUT THE AUTHOR

RAND C. LEWIS is a U.S. Army Foreign Area Officer with a specialty in Western Europe. He received his Ph.D. from the University of Idaho and has lectured and written in the areas of terrorism and issues dealing with U.S. military assistance. In the fall of 1991, he became Professor of Military Science at Duquesne University in Pittsburgh, Pennsylvania. Dr. Lewis has traveled extensively in Europe and lived in Germany, where he became interested in studying terrorism due to the history of terrorist activities within the Federal Republic of Germany.